Writing Preparation and Practice

1

Karen Blanchard   **Christine Root**

PEARSON
Longman

Writing Preparation and Practice 1

Writing Preparation and Practice 1 has been adapted by Fanny Safier from *Get Ready to Write, Second Edition*. Ms. Safier has taught literature and composition at the secondary and college levels. She has more than thirty years of experience in editing and developing middle school and secondary language arts programs.

Pearson Education, 10 Bank Street, White Plains, NY 10606

Staff credits: The people who made up the **Writing Preparation and Practice 1** team, representing editorial, production, design, and manufacturing, are John Barnes, Nancy Flaggman, Laura Le Dréan, Melissa Leyva, Jane Townsend, Paula Van Ells, and Patricia Wosczyk.

Cover image: Marjory Dressier Photo Graphics
Text composition: Rainbow Graphics
Text font: 11/14 ITC Franklin Book Gothic
Text art: Rainbow Graphics
Illustrations: James Yamasaki

Photo credits: p. 36: Stockdisc/Getty Images; p. 56: (left) Royalty-Free/Corbis, (right) Jeff Greenberg/Photo Edit; p. 76: © Muller/Gull/Getty Images; p. 81: © Charles C. Ebbets/Bettmann/Corbis; p. 82: (top) Zach Holmes/Alamy, (bottom) Ken McGraw/Index Stock Imagery; p. 83: SuperStock, Inc./SuperStock; p. 85: © Sally A. Morgan; Ecoscene/Corbis; p. 96: David De Lossy/Getty Images; p. 104: © Benjamin Rondel/Corbis; p. 105: Bettmann/Corbis; p. 107: © Reuters/Corbis; p. 109: Bettmann/Corbis; p. 111: (top) © Hamilton/Associated Press, (bottom) © Reuters/Corbis; p. 126: © Randy Faris/Corbis.

Library of Congress Cataloging-in-Publication Data

Blanchard, Karen Lourie
    Writing preparation and practice / Karen Blanchard and Christine Root.—1st ed.
        p. cm.
    ISBN 0-13-238002-1 (student book 1: alk. paper)—ISBN 0-13-199556-1 (student book 2: alk. paper)—ISBN 0-13-243553-5 (student book 3: alk. paper)   1. English language—Textbooks for foreign speakers.   2. English language—Rhetoric—Problems, exercises, etc.   3. Report writing—Problems, exercises, etc.   I. Root, Christine Baker. II. Title.
PE1128.B5875 2006
808'.0428—dc22

                                                                                2006005371

LONGMAN ON THE **WEB**

Longman.com offers online resources for teachers and students. Access our Companion Websites, our online catalog, and our local offices around the world.

Visit us at **longman.com.**

ISBN 0-13-238002-1

Printed in the United States of America
1 2 3 4 5 6 7 8 9 10—VHG—10 09 08 07 06

CONTENTS

INTRODUCTION

Writing Preparation and Practice 1 is a beginning-level writing skills textbook for English language learners who have some limited knowledge of both written and spoken English. The book is designed to acquaint students with the basic skills required for good writing and to help them become comfortable, confident, and independent writers in English.

APPROACH

Although it is a writing text, *Writing Preparation and Practice 1* integrates reading, speaking, and listening skills with prewriting, planning, and rewriting. Throughout the *Writing Preparation and Practice* series, students are called upon to write frequently and on a broad range of topics. This first book in the series is based on the premise that students at this level can and want to express themselves in English. What they need in order to do so effectively is an ever-expanding vocabulary base and successive opportunities to write short, confidence-building pieces.

Writing Preparation and Practice 1 introduces, without being overly didactic, the basic skills required for good writing in English. Through an abundance of pair and group activities as well as individual writing tasks, students learn the fundamental principles of prewriting, planning, drafting, revising, and editing as they move from sentence-level writing to guided paragraphs and beyond. Having students write early and often instills in them the confidence necessary for successful writing.

FEATURES

- Useful word banks
- Model paragraphs
- Guided practice in the stages of paragraph writing
- Grammar practice
- Sentence practice
- Paragraph pointers
- Real-life writing activities
- Topics for less structured writing
- Editing exercises with a specific grammar focus
- Ideas for students to create a portfolio of their writings

Together, the approach and features of *Writing Preparation and Practice 1* work to guide students to a higher level of confidence and proficiency.

CHAPTER 1

Introducing Yourself

Getting Ready to Write about Yourself

Learning to write in a new language is not always easy. It can be hard, but it can also be fun. If you are learning to speak and read in a new language, you are ready to begin writing, too.

The easiest way to begin writing is to write about things you know well. That often means writing about yourself.

As you complete the exercises in *Writing Preparation and Practice 1*, you will do a lot of writing about yourself and your life. You will find it interesting and helpful to keep your writing in a special folder called a *portfolio*.

MAKE A COVER FOR YOUR PORTFOLIO

A Look at the cover that a student designed for his portfolio.

B Design the cover for your own portfolio on a separate piece of paper. Use drawings, pictures, and words to describe who you are. Here are some suggestions for things to include:

- Your family and friends
- Your interests and favorite activities
- Sports you like to play or watch

- Your travel experiences
- Books or movies you have enjoyed
- Your favorite places, foods, holidays

C Put your design on the cover of your portfolio.

D Share the cover of your portfolio with your classmates.

- Show and explain the cover of your portfolio.

- Write your name on the chalkboard and teach your classmates how to pronounce it.

- Does your name have a special meaning in your language? What does it mean?

- Tell your classmates what language(s) you speak. Also tell them why you are studying English.

Word Bank			
Arabic	German	Japanese	Romanian
Cantonese	Greek	Korean	Russian
Czech	Hebrew	Mandarin	Spanish
Dutch	Indonesian	Polish	Thai
French	Italian	Portuguese	Vietnamese

Developing Your Writing Skills

WHAT IS A SENTENCE?

An English sentence always has a subject and a verb. Many sentences have an object, too. The most common order for English sentences is subject + verb + object.

The subject is a noun or pronoun. It is usually a person or thing that is doing the action. The verb tells the action. The object is also a noun or pronoun. It usually answers the question "what or who(m)."

> **EXAMPLES**
>
> | Anna | speaks | Russian. |
> |---|---|---|
> | (subject) | (verb) | (object) |
>
> | Paulo | plays | soccer. |
> |---|---|---|
> | (subject) | (verb) | (object) |

Most verbs, like *play*, *read*, *give*, *speak*, describe an action. A few other verbs called linking verbs are not action verbs. The most common linking verb is *be*. Sentences with linking verbs are followed by adjectives or nouns. These adjectives and nouns always tell us something about the subject of a sentence. They are called *complements*. (You will learn about adjectives in Chapters 2 and 5.)

EXAMPLES

Anna	is	happy.
(subject)	(linking verb)	(complement)

Paulo	is	a teacher.
(subject)	(linking verb)	(complement)

A sentence may contain more than a single subject, verb, object, or complement.

EXAMPLES

Anna and Paulo are classmates.
(compound subject)

Anna wrote and revised her report.
(compound verb)

Paulo checked the library and bookstore.
(compound object)

They were happy and eager.
(compound complement)

Circle the verb in each sentence. Underline the subject. Draw a box around the object or complement.

EXAMPLE

Mr. Robertson (is) tired .

1. Chris kicked the soccer ball.

2. She is shy.

3. Andrea and Marshall ride bikes.

4. He is a banker.

5. We watch movies.

6. They are funny.

PREWRITING

Before you begin writing, it is helpful to think about, talk about, or make notes about your ideas. Prewriting is one step in the process of writing.

Answer these questions about yourself in complete sentences.

1. What is your name?

_____

2. Where are you from?

_____

3. What language or languages do you speak?

_____

4. What subjects are you studying in school?

_____

5. What do you like to do? (For example, do you like to go to the movies? Do you like to read magazines? Do you like to listen to music? Do you like to go shopping?)

_____

CAPITAL LETTERS

The first word of every sentence begins with a capital letter. Other important words in English begin with a capital letter, too. Follow these rules for using capital letters.

Rules	Examples
1. The first word of a sentence or question	**W**hat is his name? **H**is name is Ernesto Reyes.
2. The pronoun *I*	Harris and **I** like to play tennis together.
3. The names and titles of people	He has an appointment with **D**r. **C**arol **W**olf. Let's call **S**ong **Y**ee.
4. The names of countries, cities, states, continents, and streets	They live in **L**ima, **P**eru. **P**eru is in **S**outh **A**merica. She is from **A**ustin, **T**exas. The library is on **J**uniper **S**treet.
5. Days of the week and months of the year	His birthday is next **T**hursday. We're going on vacation in **J**une.
6. The names of languages and nationalities	He speaks **V**ietnamese. My grandparents are **M**exican.

Rewrite each sentence. Add the capital letters.

1. i like to travel.

_____

2. yumi lives in tokyo, japan.

_____

3. when did they get back from mexico?

_____

4. mr. kim has a meeting on friday.

_____

5. ali is studying spanish and english this semester.

_____

6. my birthday is in july.

_____

7. what do you want to do on sunday?

_____

WHAT IS A PARAGRAPH?

Most English writing is organized into paragraphs. You will write many paragraphs in this book. A paragraph is a group of sentences about one main idea. This main idea is called the *topic*.

An English paragraph has a special form. Read the paragraph below. It is written in the correct form.

Capital letter

Begin next sentence here.

Indent

Period

My name is Ernesto Reyes. I am from Taxco, Mexico. I am fifteen years old. I speak Spanish and English. I want to be an engineer. I love sports, especially basketball, soccer, scuba diving, and ultimate Frisbee. I also like to travel and go to parties.

1. Indent the first line of each new paragraph about 2 centimeters (¾ of an inch) from the margin.
2. Begin each sentence with a capital letter.
3. End each sentence with a period.
4. Do not start each new sentence on a new line.

A Look at the paragraph. Get together with a partner, and talk about what is wrong with its form.

my name is Lilly Lang

I am twenty-eight years old

I am from Atlanta, Georgia

my native language is English

I am an artist.

B Write the paragraph in the correct form.

_____

_____

_____

_____

_____

WRITING

Writing is the step that follows prewriting in the writing process (see page 4). In this part of the process, you use ideas that you developed earlier.

Use the sentences you wrote about yourself on page 5 to write a paragraph about yourself on the lines below. Follow the rules of paragraph writing.

My name is _____

_____

_____

_____

_____

REVISING

Revising is another step in the process of writing. In revising, you make corrections and changes in your writing.

A Exchange paragraphs with a partner. Read your partner's paragraph and check *yes* or *no* for each question on the Paragraph Checklist. Then help your partner improve his/her paragraph.

PARAGRAPH CHECKLIST	YES	NO
1. Is the first word of the paragraph indented?	❏	❏
2. Does each sentence begin with a capital letter?	❏	❏
3. Does each sentence end with a period?	❏	❏
4. Does each new sentence begin next to the one before it?	❏	❏

B Use your partner's suggestions to revise your paragraph. Copy it onto a separate piece of paper. Give it the title "About Me" and put it in your portfolio.

PREWRITING

A Talk to a classmate. Ask him/her these questions. Write short answers on the lines.

1. What is your name?

_____

2. Where are you from?

_____

3. What is your native language?

_____

4. What subjects are you studying in school?

_____

5. What do you like to do?

_____

6. What else do you like to do?

_____

B Use the answers to complete the sentences about your classmate. Then copy the complete sentence on the line.

> EXAMPLE
>
> My classmate's name is _Oscar_____.
> _My classmate's name is Oscar._

1. My classmate's name is _____.

   _____

2. He/She is from _____.

   _____

3. He/She speaks _____.

   _____

4. He/She is studying _____.

   _____

5. He/She likes to _____.

   _____

6. He/She also likes to _____.

   _____

WRITING

Use your sentences to write a paragraph about your classmate. Remember to follow the rules of paragraph writing.

My classmate's name is _____

_____

_____

_____

_____

REVISING

A Exchange paragraphs with your partner. Read the paragraph your partner wrote about you. Make sure the information about you is correct. Then use the Paragraph Checklist to help your partner improve his/her paragraph.

B Use your partner's suggestions to revise your paragraph. Copy it onto a separate piece of paper and give it the title "My Classmate." Share your paragraph with your classmates. Put it in your portfolio.

On Your Own

Write a paragraph about your teacher or another one of your classmates. Use the Prewriting questions on page 8 to help you get started. Show your paragraph to a partner and use the Paragraph Checklist on page 8 to improve your paragraph.

You Be the Editor

The paragraph "A Lucky and Happy Man" has eight mistakes in the use of capital letters. With a partner, find the mistakes and correct them.

A Lucky and Happy Man

My name is Stanley stoico. I am ninety years old. I am from italy. I moved to San Diego, california, with my family when I was nine years old. I speak italian and english. in my younger years, I had many different jobs. I worked hard and saved my money. In 1955, I started my own business. the business was successful, and i retired in 1983. I like to travel and play golf. I have seen and done a lot in my long life. I am a lucky and happy man.

FILLING OUT A FORM

Fill out the form with information about yourself.

Student Information Form

Please print.

1. Name: _____
         Last   First   Middle

2. Address: _____

   _____

3. Phone Number: _____ E-mail: _____

4. Sex: _____ M _____ F

5. Age: _____

6. Nationality: _____

7. First Language: _____

8. Other Languages: _____

9. How long have you studied English? (Please check one.)

   _____ Never

   _____ Less than 1 year

   _____ 1–2 years

   _____ More than 2 years

10. Do you work? _____ Yes _____ No

11. If yes, where? _____ What hours? _____

12. Signature: _____

CHAPTER 2

Writing about Your Family and Friends

Getting Ready to Write about Family

A A family tree is a chart that shows the generations of people in a family. Look at Tom Brower's family tree. Then ask and answer the questions with a partner. Use the words in the Word Bank on the next page to help you.

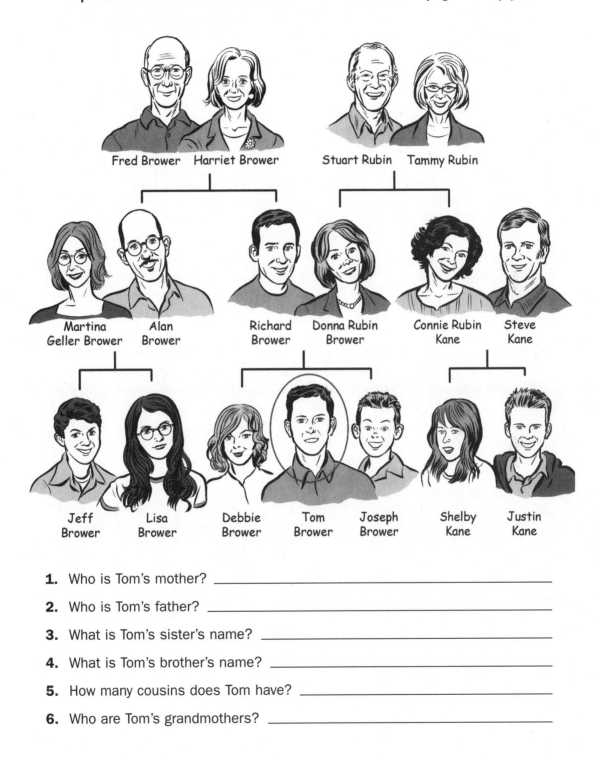

1. Who is Tom's mother? _____

2. Who is Tom's father? _____

3. What is Tom's sister's name? _____

4. What is Tom's brother's name? _____

5. How many cousins does Tom have? _____

6. Who are Tom's grandmothers? _____

Word Bank

aunt	granddaughter	married	son
brother	grandfather	mother	stepfather
child/children	grandmother	nephew	stepsister
cousin	grandson	niece	uncle
daughter	great-grandfather	parents	wife
divorced	great-grandmother	single	
father	husband	sister	

B Read the paragraph Tom wrote about his family.

> I have a big family, and we all get along very well. My parents' names are Richard and Donna Brower. I have one younger brother. His name is Joseph. He is ten years old. I also have an older sister. Her name is Debbie. She is nineteen years old. I have four cousins. Their names are Jeff Brower, Lisa Brower, Shelby Kane, and Justin Kane. I usually see them on the weekends. My grandparents love to invite us to their house for dinner. My family always has a great time together.

C On a separate piece of paper, draw your own family tree. Give it the title "My Family Tree" and put it in your portfolio. You may illustrate your family tree with drawings or photographs.

If you prefer, you may choose a historical figure and draw his or her family tree.

Developing Your Writing Skills

SUBJECT AND OBJECT PRONOUNS

Pronouns are used to refer to a noun that has already been mentioned. Pronouns help you connect sentences without repeating the same nouns. Pronouns can be singular or plural. Two of the most common kinds of pronouns are subject pronouns and object pronouns.

SUBJECT PRONOUNS

Subject pronouns (such as *we*, *she*, *they*) serve as the subject of a sentence.

Debbie is my sister. **She** is eighteen years old. (She = Debbie)
                    (subject)
Abdullah is my cousin. **He** works at a bank. (He = Abdullah)
                    (subject)

Singular (one person/thing)	Plural (two or more people/things)
I	we
you	you
he, she, it	they

A Underline the subject pronouns in the paragraph about Tom's family on page 14.

B Complete the second sentence in each pair with a subject pronoun.

1. <u>Mrs. Gonzalez</u> is a teacher. _____ teaches English.

2. <u>My car</u> is green. _____ is new.

3. <u>John and I</u> are brothers. _____ are both students.

4. <u>Amy and Gladys</u> are cousins. _____ live in Taiwan.

5. <u>Jorge</u> loves sports. _____ plays basketball, soccer, and golf.

OBJECT PRONOUNS

Object pronouns serve as the object of a verb.

Fran called *Mrs. Davis*. Fran called **her**. (her = Mrs. Davis)
                    (object)
David e-mailed *Stan* and *Joey*. David e-mailed **them**. (them = Stan and Joey)
                    (object)

Singular	Plural
me	us
you	you
him, her, it	them

C Circle the object pronouns in the paragraph about Tom's family on page 14.

D Complete the second sentence in each pair with an object pronoun.

1. We called <u>Mr. Smith</u>. We called _____.

2. I drove <u>my mother</u> to the station. I drove _____ to the station.

3. Pam misses <u>her little boy</u>. Pam misses _____.

4. We e-mailed <u>our friends</u> last week. We e-mailed _____ last week.

POSSESSIVE ADJECTIVES

Possessive adjectives modify nouns to show ownership.

> EXAMPLES
>
> **My** sisters are very close.
> Drew is selling **his** car.
> The Ortegas painted **their** apartment.
> Donna smiled at **her** mother.

Singular	Plural
my	our
your	your
his, her, its	their

A Draw a box around the possessive adjectives in the paragraph about Tom's family on page 14.

B Complete each sentence with the correct possessive adjective.

1. I like to spend time with _____ brothers.

2. My sister loves _____ new puppy.

3. My parents love _____ children.

4. Daniel likes to play games on _____ computer.

5. Suzanne and Gary enjoy playing with _____ cousins.

C Complete the paragraph with the correct pronoun or possessive adjective.

My Grandparents' Album

I love to look at ___*my*___ (me, my) grandparents' old photograph
                        1.

album. It is always fun to see pictures of _____ (me, my) mother
                                             2.

when _____ (she, her) was a little girl. _____ (She, Her) looks
       3.   4.

so cute with _____ (she, her) curly hair and big smile. I also like
              5.

looking at all of the different cars my grandfather bought over the

years. _____ (He, Him) loved _____ (him, his) cars, and he
        6.   7.

took very good care of _____ (they, them). My favorite pictures are
                        8.

the ones of _____ (me, my) parents' wedding. My mother and
             9.

father look nervous, but I am sure _____ (them, they) were very
                                    10.

happy. The last part of the album is filled with pictures of _____
                                                              11.

(my, me) and _____ (my, me) baby brother. I think I look like my
              12.

mother when she was _____ (my, me) age. I am so glad my
                      13.

grandparents made this album.

PREWRITING

A Answer these questions about your family.

1. How many people are there in your family? _____

2. What are your parents' names? _____

Where do they live? _____

3. What does your father do? _____

What does your mother do? _____

4. How many brothers and sisters do you have? _____

What are their names? _____ How old are they?

_____

5. Do you have any cousins? _____ How many?

_____ What are their names? _____

How old are they? _____

B Write at least five sentences about your family.

1. _____

2. _____

3. _____

4. _____

5. _____

WRITING

Use your sentences to write a paragraph about your family. Begin by choosing an adjective (a descriptive word such as *big, small, happy*) to complete the first sentence. Remember to follow the rules of paragraph writing. Use at least five pronouns in your paragraph.

I have a _____ *family.*
        (big/small/happy)

_____

_____

_____

_____

_____

REVISING

A Exchange paragraphs with a partner. Read your partner's paragraph and check *yes* or *no* for each question on the Paragraph Checklist. Then help your partner improve his/her paragraph.

PARAGRAPH CHECKLIST		
	YES	NO
1. Is the first word of the paragraph indented?	❑	❑
2. Does each sentence begin with a capital letter and end with a period?	❑	❑
3. Does each new sentence begin next to the one before it?	❑	❑
4. Are there at least five pronouns?	❑	❑

B Use your partner's suggestions to revise your paragraph. Copy it onto a separate piece of paper. Give it the title "My Family" and put it in your portfolio.

PREWRITING

A Think of a relative you would like to write about.

Write his/her name here. _____

B Answer the questions about him/her.

1. How is this person related to you (a cousin/aunt/grandparent)? _____
2. How old is he/she? _____
3. Is he/she married or single? _____
4. Where does he/she live? _____
5. What does he/she do? _____
6. What does he/she like to do? _____

C Add one or two more interesting things about him/her.

_____

_____

WRITING

Use your sentences to write a paragraph about someone in your family. Use at least five pronouns in your paragraph.

_My_ _____ _'s name is_ _____ . _____

_____

_____

_____

_____

REVISING

A Exchange paragraphs with a partner. Read your partner's paragraph and check *yes* or *no* for each question on the Paragraph Checklist. Then help your partner improve his/her paragraph.

PARAGRAPH CHECKLIST

		YES	NO
1.	Is the first word of the paragraph indented?	❑	❑
2.	Does each sentence begin with a capital letter and end with a period?	❑	❑
3.	Does each new sentence begin next to the one before it?	❑	❑
4.	Are there at least five pronouns?	❑	❑

B Use your partner's suggestions to revise your paragraph. Then copy it onto a separate piece of paper. Give it the title "My _____" (Example: "My Brother") and put it in your portfolio.

USING *AND, BUT,* OR *SO*

When you write in English you can combine sentences using the words *and*, *but*, and *so* to make your writing more interesting. These words are called *conjunctions*.

Conjunction	Use	Example
and	joins two similar ideas together	Enzo Ricordi has a close family, **and** he loves them very much.
but	joins two contrasting ideas	He enjoys spending time with them, **but** he doesn't get to see them very much.
so	shows that the second idea is the result of the first	Enzo misses his family, **so** he keeps a photograph of the whole family in his wallet.

A Combine the pairs of sentences using *and*, *but*, or *so*.

1. Sandra goes out with her cousins. She goes out with her friends, too.

_____

2. Maria would like to spend more time with her sisters. She is usually too busy.

_____

3. Erin wants to e-mail her mother. Her computer is broken.

_____

4. Min misses her brother. She calls him almost every day.

_____

5. Ana doesn't have enough money to buy a new computer. She got a part-time job.

_____

B Compare your sentences with a partner's. Did you use the same words to combine the sentences?

C Read the paragraph below and circle the conjunctions.

I have a good friend, José, and he is like a brother to me. He is very responsible, but he is also fun to be with. We enjoy getting together. He is smart and reads a lot, so he always has interesting things to say. He is quite a talkative guy, but he is a very good listener, too. I can talk about my problems with him, and he always gives me good advice. I am really glad to have a friend like José.

PARAGARAPH POINTER **The Writing Process**

Writing a paragraph is a process that includes several steps. The steps in the process are called prewriting, writing, and revising. (See pages 4, 7, and 8.) When you follow the steps, it will be easier to write a good paragraph.

Step One: Prewriting
Before you write a paragraph, it is helpful to think, talk, and make lists of ideas about the topic. This gets you ready to write.

Step Two: Writing
Use your prewriting ideas to help you write your paragraph.

Step Three: Revising
Make corrections and changes in your paragraph.

PREWRITING

A In small groups, discuss the qualities of a good friend. Put a check next to the qualities that you think are important.

1. _____ responsible   **5.** _____ good listener   **8.** _____ wealthy

2. _____ fun to be with   **6.** _____ honest   **9.** _____ loyal

3. _____ kind   **7.** _____ good-looking   **10.** _____ warm

4. _____ intelligent

B Choose a friend that you would like to write about and describe your friend to the people in your group.

Write his/her name here. _____

C Fill in the information about your friend.

1. How old is your friend? _____

2. Where does he/she live? _____

3. What language(s) does he/she speak? _____

4. What does he/she like to do? _____

5. What words would you use to describe your friend? _____

_____

D Add one or two more interesting facts about your friend.

_____

_____

WRITING

Use some of your sentences to write a paragraph about your friend. Remember to follow the rules of paragraph writing. Use at least five pronouns in your paragraph.

My friend's name is _____. _____

_____

_____

_____

_____

A Exchange paragraphs with a partner. Read your partner's paragraph and check *yes* or *no* for each question on the Paragraph Checklist. Then help your partner improve his/her paragraph.

PARAGRAPH CHECKLIST

		YES	NO
1.	Is the first word of the paragraph indented?	❏	❏
2.	Does each sentence begin with a capital letter and end with a period?	❏	❏
3.	Does each new sentence begin next to the one before it?	❏	❏
4.	Are there at least five pronouns?	❏	❏

B Use your partner's suggestions to revise your paragraph. Copy it onto a separate piece of paper. Give it the title "My Friend _____" and put it in your portfolio.

On Your Own

Write a paragraph about another friend or a family member. Use the questions on page 22 to help you get started. Show your paragraph to a partner and use the Paragraph Checklist to improve your paragraph.

Using Your Imagination

A Pretend it is the year 2025. Make a list of sentences about your family.

EXAMPLES

I have a son named Stephen. He is getting married next week.

My daughter's name is Diana. She is the mayor of my hometown.

1. _____

2. _____

3. _____

4. _____

5. _____

B Choose an adjective—a descriptive word such as *wonderful, small, large,* or *unusual*—to describe your "future" family and complete the first sentence. Then use your sentences to write a paragraph.

I have a _____ *family.* _____

_____

_____

_____

_____

_____

You Be the Editor

The paragraph "My Cousin" has five mistakes in the use of pronouns. With a partner, find the mistakes and correct them.

My Cousin

My cousin's name is Bettina Lee. She is twenty-seven years old. She was born in Chicago, Illinois, but now her lives in Denver, Colorado. She is married and has two children. Bettina and me enjoy spending time together. Us love to go ice-skating. Bettina is an excellent ice-skater. She skated in ice shows when he was young. Now Bettina teaches ice-skating to young children. She enjoys watching their.

Real-Life Writing

WRITING AN E-MAIL MESSAGE

Writing e-mail messages is a quick and easy way to communicate. E-mails are usually short and specific.

A Read the sample e-mail.

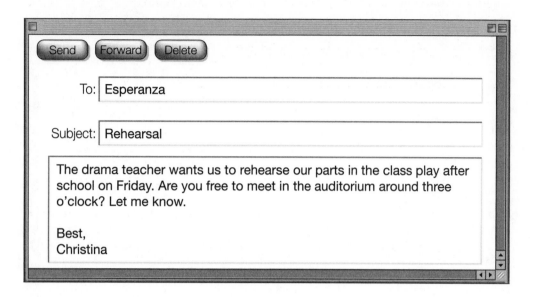

Send   Forward   Delete

To: Esperanza

Subject: Rehearsal

The drama teacher wants us to rehearse our parts in the class play after school on Friday. Are you free to meet in the auditorium around three o'clock? Let me know.

Best,
Christina

B Write an e-mail for each of the situations.

1. Write an e-mail to your cousin Juanita. Remind her to stop at the pizza shop on her way to your home and get a large mushroom pizza.

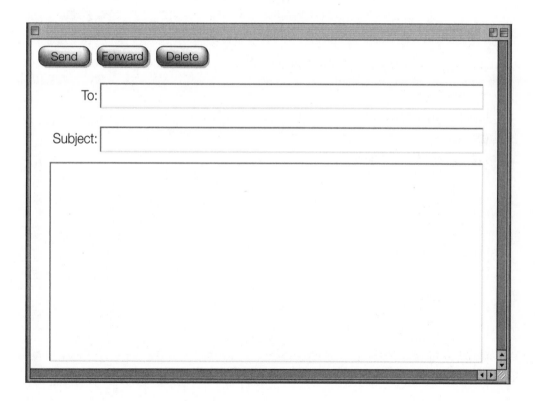

Send   Forward   Delete

To:

Subject:

2. Write an e-mail to your friend Julio. Tell him that you are sorry, but you will not be able to meet him for a chess lesson tonight. Ask him if tomorrow night is good for him.

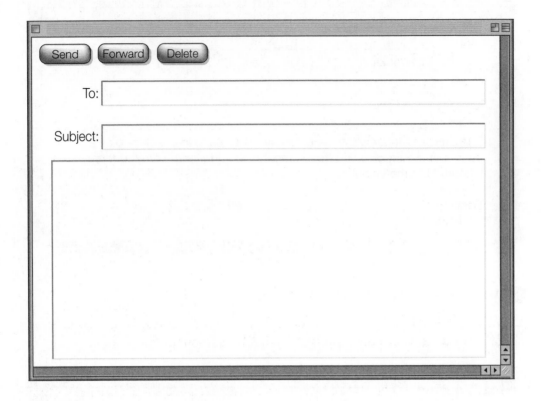

3. Write an e-mail to your coach. Tell him you hurt your ankle and can't come to the practice session tomorrow.

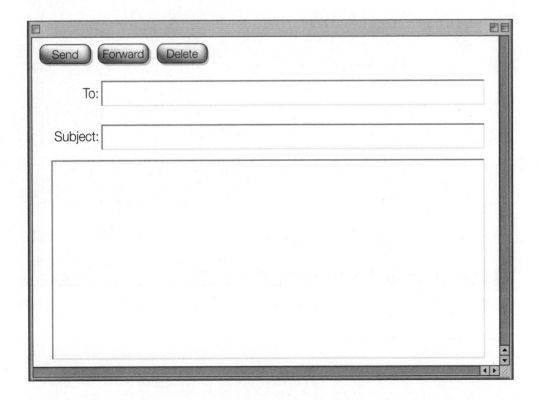

CHAPTER 3

Writing about Your Activities

Getting Ready to Write about Your Activities

A Look at the five pictures. They show the things a student named Eric likes to do with his friends. Write the name of the activity under the correct picture. Use the words in the Word Bank.

> **Word Bank**
>
> buying CDs   listening to music   playing soccer
>
> going to the movies   playing computer games

1. _____

2. _____

3. _____

4. _____

5. _____

B Complete the paragraph below with words from the Word Bank above. Be sure to use the correct form of the verb.

Spending Time with Friends

When he has free time, Eric enjoys spending time with his friends.

They often _____ soccer together after class. They also

                       1.

like playing computer _____ and going to the

                                  2.

_____ together. Eric and his friends like

_____ to music, so they often go to the music store to
  4.

_____ new CDs. Sometimes they don't go anywhere, but
  5.

they aren't bored. They just sit around and talk and laugh. Eric and his

friends always have fun when they are together.

C **Talk to a partner. Ask and answer these questions.**

1. What does Eric like to do in his free time?

2. What sport does Eric like to play with his friends?

3. What else does Eric like to do with his friends?

Developing Your Writing Skills

THE SIMPLE PRESENT TENSE

The tense of a verb indicates time.

> EXAMPLES
>
> I *live* in Ohio. (present)
> Last year I *lived* in New Jersey. (past)

Single-word verbs are used for the simple present tense.

Verbs in the simple present tense have two forms: the *s* form and the base form.
The form of the verb that you use depends on the subject of the sentence.

1. The *s* Form: When the subject is a singular noun (*Cathy, the car, the dog,*
etc.) or a singular pronoun (*he, she, or it*), add *s* (or *es* or *ies*) to the verb.

2. The Base Form: When the subject is a plural noun (*Cathy and Tom, the
cars, the dogs,* etc.) or one of the other pronouns (*I, you, we, they*), use
the base form of the verb. Do not add *s*.

In the following examples, the base forms are *enjoy* and *like*.

> EXAMPLES
>
> Eric *enjoys* spending time with his friends. He *likes* to play computer games
> with them.
> I *enjoy* spending time with my friends. I *like* to go shopping with them.

Spelling Rules for Forming the *s* Form of the Simple Present Tense	Examples
1. For most verbs, add *s*	work—works play—plays
2. For verbs ending in consonant + *y*, change the *y* to *i* and add *es*	worry—worries
3. For verbs ending in *s, z, ch, sh, x*, add *es*	catch—catches
4. Irregular verbs	go—goes do—does have—has

The verb *be* has its own form in the present tense:

I ***am*** | he
she
it } ***is*** | they
you
we } ***are***

A **The sentences have mistakes in the use of the simple present tense verbs. Correct the mistakes.**

1. Maria worrys about her children.

2. We plays soccer on the weekend.

3. You is never on time.

4. She wash her clothes at the laundromat.

5. Both of my sisters lives in Texas.

6. I has lots of new friends in my class.

7. I think he watchs too much TV.

B Rewrite the paragraph. Change *I* to *Hector* in the first sentence. Make all the necessary changes.

A Newspaper Delivery Job

I have a newspaper route. Every morning before I go to class, I deliver the local newspaper to families in my neighborhood. Most days I ride my bicycle. I place the newspapers in a basket that I attach to my handlebars. When it snows, I walk and carry the newspapers in a large backpack. I am happy to have this job. I plan to buy a cell phone with the money I earn.

Hector has _____

_____

_____

_____

_____

_____

_____

PARTS OF A PARAGRAPH IN ENGLISH

> **PARAGARAPH POINTER** **Parts of a Paragraph**
>
> Most paragraphs have three main parts:
> **1.** A topic sentence
> **2.** Several supporting sentences
> **3.** A concluding sentence

1. The *topic sentence* is the most important sentence in the paragraph. It is often, but not always, the first sentence in the paragraph. The topic sentence tells the reader what the paragraph is about.

2. Next come the *supporting sentences*. These sentences give details, examples, and reasons to explain the topic sentence. All of the supporting sentences must relate to the topic of the paragraph.

3. Some paragraphs end with a *concluding sentence.* The concluding sentence restates the main idea in different words. Here are some common ways to begin a concluding sentence:

All in all,   As you can see,   In conclusion,

Work with a partner. Read each paragraph and identify the parts. Ask and answer the questions that follow.

1. Serita likes to spend her free time as a volunteer at the local community center. She reads stories to a group of preschool children and plays games with them. When senior citizens play Bingo, she helps to call out the numbers. She also assists in the reading room by locating books for readers and keeping the bookshelves in order. As you can see, Serita enjoys using her free time to help others.

   a. What is the topic sentence?

   b. How many supporting sentences are there?

   c. What is the concluding sentence?

2. I have several hobbies that keep me busy in my free time. I love to read, and I often read short stories and magazines. Another one of my hobbies is cooking, and Chinese cooking is my specialty. My favorite hobby is photography. I usually take black and white pictures because I think they are more interesting. In conclusion, without my hobbies, my life would not be as much fun.

   a. What is the topic sentence?

   b. How many supporting sentences are there?

   c. What is the concluding sentence?

USING *WHEN*

You can use *when* to show that two things happen at the same time.

> EXAMPLES
>
>   Eric and his friends always have fun **when** they are together.
>   **When** they are together, Eric and his friends always have fun.

Notice that we use a comma in sentences that start with *when*.

A Combine the pairs of sentences using *when*. Use a comma.

1. I'm bored. I call my friends.

   _____

2. My friends come over. We play video games.

   _____

3. I don't exercise. I feel very tired.

_____

4. I go running. I have a lot of energy.

_____

B Complete the sentences. Then compare your sentences with those of a partner.

1. When I wake up in the morning, I _____.

2. When I get to school, I _____.

3. When I feel tired, I _____.

4. When I exercise, I _____.

PREWRITING

A What do you like to do in your free time? Talk to a partner. Discuss some things that you like to do with your friends or family. Use the Word Bank to help you with vocabulary.

Word Bank			
bake	go to museums	play guitar/ piano	spend time online
cook	go to parties		swim
dance	go to the movies	play soccer	take pictures
draw	listen to music	play tennis	take walks
exercise/ work out	paint	read	talk on the phone
	play chess	sew	travel
go shopping	play computer/ video games	sing	watch TV
go to concerts		ski	

B Make a list of the things you like to do.

_____   _____

_____   _____

_____   _____

_____   _____

C Share your list with your partner. Talk about the things you like to do the most. Do you and your partner like to do any of the same things? Which ones?

D Use your list to complete each of the sentences.

1. I like to _____.

2. I also like to _____.

3. Another thing I enjoy is _____.

4. I like to _____, and I _____.

5. I enjoy _____, but I _____.

WRITING

Use your sentences to write a paragraph. Complete the topic sentence. Include at least four supporting sentences. Complete the concluding sentence.

When I have free time, I _____

_____

_____

_____

As you can see, _____

REVISING

A Exchange paragraphs with a partner. Read your partner's paragraph and check *yes* or *no* for each question on the Paragraph Checklist. Then help your partner improve his/her paragraph.

PARAGRAPH CHECKLIST	YES	NO
1. Does each sentence begin with a capital letter and end with a period?	❑	❑
2. Does each new sentence begin next to the one before it?	❑	❑
3. Is there a topic sentence?	❑	❑
4. Are there at least four supporting sentences?	❑	❑
5. Is there a concluding sentence?	❑	❑

B Use your partner's suggestions to revise your paragraph. Copy it onto a separate piece of paper. Give it the title "My Free Time" and put it in your portfolio.

WRITING ABOUT KEEPING FIT

A Lots of people like to exercise to stay healthy. Look at the pictures of people exercising. Complete the sentences. Use the words in the Word Bank.

Word Bank		
aerobic dancing	karate	swimming
bike	lifts weights	walking
cross-country skiing	running	yoga

1. Jason gets a lot of exercise when he goes _____.

2. Marsha _____ three times a week.

3. Julio goes _____ every day after school.

4. Mark rides his _____ to school for exercise.

5. Alice takes _____ classes at her gym.

6. _____ is David's favorite kind of exercise.

7. Mr. Wolf goes

_____

before dinner to
exercise.

8. Hannah does

_____

to relax.

9. Ian practices

_____

once a week.

B Study the vocabulary in the Word Bank. Then read the paragraph "Keeping Fit" and answer the questions.

Word Bank			
exercise	health club	stay healthy	track
gym	keep fit	stay in shape	work out

Keeping Fit

Steve Fredericks cares about keeping fit. First of all, he tries to get some exercise every day. He belongs to a health club, where he usually exercises after work. He likes to lift weights and run on the track. In addition, he is careful about his diet. For example, he rarely eats foods that have a lot of fat or sugar. Finally, Steve tries to get eight hours of sleep every night. Like many of his friends, Steve tries to keep in shape and stay healthy.

1. What is the topic sentence?

_____

2. What are three things that Steve does to support the fact that he cares about keeping fit?

_____

_____

_____

3. What is the concluding sentence?

_____

PREWRITING

A Answer each question in a complete sentence. Then discuss your answers with a partner.

1. What kind of exercise do you enjoy?

_____

2. How often do you exercise?

_____

3. Do you eat well-balanced meals?

_____

4. Do you usually get enough sleep at night? How many hours of sleep do you usually get? How much sleep do you need?

_____

_____

5. How do you usually feel after you exercise: energetic, relaxed, tired, or hungry?

_____

B Work with a group of three or four students. Make a list of seven ways to stay healthy. Write your ideas in the chart.

Ways to Stay Healthy
1. *Read the labels on food products to learn what ingredients are included.*
2.
3.
4.
5.
6.
7.

C Compare your chart with another group's. Did you have any of the same ideas? Which ones were the same?

WRITING

Complete the paragraph about the things you do to stay healthy. The topic sentence is given. Use some of the ideas from your chart for the supporting sentences. End your paragraph with a concluding sentence.

I do several things to try to stay healthy.

_____

_____

_____

_____

REVISING

A Exchange paragraphs with a partner. Read your partner's paragraph and check *yes* or *no* for each question on the Paragraph Checklist. Then help your partner improve his/her paragraph.

PARAGRAPH CHECKLIST	YES	NO
1. Does each sentence begin with a capital letter and end with a period?	❏	❏
2. Does each new sentence begin next to the one before it?	❏	❏
3. Is there a topic sentence?	❏	❏
4. Are there at least three supporting sentences?	❏	❏
5. Is there a concluding sentence?	❏	❏

B Use your partner's suggestions to revise your paragraph. Copy it onto a separate piece of paper. Give it the title "Staying Healthy" and put it in your portfolio.

On Your Own

Choose one of the topics to write about.

1. Talk to someone in your family or one of your friends about what he/she likes to do in his/her free time. Write a paragraph about how that person spends his/her free time.

2. Talk to someone in your family or one of your friends about what he/she does to stay healthy. Write a paragraph about how that person stays healthy.

You Be the Editor

The paragraph "My Busy Sister" has six mistakes in the use of simple present tense verbs. With a partner, find the six mistakes and correct them.

My Busy Sister

My sister Stephanie is always busy after school. As soon as she get home, she turnes on the TV. At the same time, she talk on the phone to make plans with her best friend. After she watchs TV and eats a snack, she playies computer games or IMs her friends for a while. Then she gos shopping with her friends. No wonder she's too tired to do her homework after dinner.

Real-Life Writing

WRITING NOTES FOR A MESSAGE BOARD

A Read the Wanted messages.

> **Wanted:**
> I need a ride to New York City on Friday, January 21. Call Mehmet at 555-7019.

> **Wanted:**
> Looking for a used tennis racket in good condition. If you have one to sell, please call Lucia at 555-0856.

> **Wanted:**
> I'm looking for someone willing to give me chess lessons in exchange for tutoring in Spanish. Call Leah at 555-1024.

B Write your own message for something you want or need.

C Read the For Sale messages.

> **For Sale:**
> Bicycle in good condition. Call Hank at
> 555-6240 for details.

> **For Sale:**
> I am selling my collection of CDs and
> DVDs. For a list of all titles and prices,
> call Joe at 555-2280 or e-mail me at
> DJ@me.com.

> **Moving!**
> Must sell cheap: 17-inch color
> TV. Three years old. Works perfectly.
> Call Marie at 555-7124.

D Write your own message for something you want to sell.

Writing about Your Day

Getting Ready to Write about Your Day

A Look at the pictures. They describe a typical day in the life of a girl named Kim Ling. Match each picture with the correct sentence. Write the number next to the sentence.

 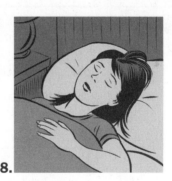

____ She attends school from 8:30 to 3:00.

____ Kim wakes up at 7:00 A.M.

____ Kim is usually asleep by 11:00 P.M.

____ Then she waits for the bus to school at 7:45 A.M.

____ At 6:00 she eats dinner with her family.

____ She rides the bus home at 3:15.

____ She practices piano from 5:00 to 6:00 P.M.

____ When she gets home at 4:00, she begins her homework.

B Use the sentences about Kim to complete a paragraph about a typical day in her life. The topic sentence and concluding sentences are given.

Kim's days are very busy. _____

_____

_____

_____

As you can see, Kim has a very busy life. _____

Developing Your Writing Skills

USING PREPOSITIONS OF TIME

It is important to use the correct preposition when you are writing about time.

A Study the chart.

Prepositions of Time	Examples
on	+ day of the week (I go to work **on** Monday.)
	+ day of the week + part of a day (I take an English class **on** Monday night.)
	+ a specific date (She was born **on** April 30.)
in	+ a month (She was born **in** April.)
	+ a part of the day (I do my homework **in** the evening.)
	Exception: **at** night (I do my homework **at** night.)
at	+ a specific time (My English class starts **at** 9:30.)
from	+ a specific time or date **to** a specific time or date (Mr. Morimoto exercises **from** 5:30 **to** 6:30 every morning.)

B Complete the sentences with the correct preposition of time.

1. Do you want to go to the movies _____ Sunday afternoon?

2. She is going to the dentist _____ Monday.

3. Mohammed goes to work _____ 9:00.

4. Cheng goes to school _____ the morning.

5. I sent the e-mail _____ January 29.

6. I like to watch TV _____ night.

7. I have classes _____ 10:00 _____ 4:30.

8. The new semester starts _____ January.

9. He wakes up _____ 7:30 _____ the morning.

10. Keiko was in the hospital _____ July 3 _____ July 7.

USING FREQUENCY ADVERBS

When you want to write about how often something happens or how often you do
something, you can use frequency adverbs in your sentences. Common frequency
adverbs are *always, usually, often, sometimes, rarely, seldom,* and *never*.

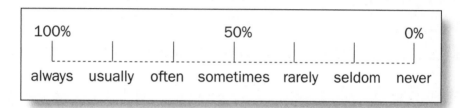

Notes about placement:

1. Frequency adverbs are used *before* regular verbs but *after* forms of the
verb **be**.

> EXAMPLES
>
> He <u>always</u> **goes** to bed late.
> He **is** <u>always</u> tired in the morning.

2. *Sometimes* can also come at the beginning of a sentence.

> EXAMPLES
>
> I <u>sometimes</u> take the bus to work.
> <u>Sometimes</u> I take the bus to work.

Adverbs	Examples
always (100% of the time)	I don't have a bus pass. I *always* walk to school.
usually	He *usually* gets up at 7:00 A.M. He is *usually* on time for class.
often	We *often* go for a walk after dinner. We are *often* tired after our walk.
sometimes (50% of the time)	I *sometimes* fall asleep in front of the television. I am *sometimes* late for basketball practice. *Sometimes* I do my homework in the morning.
rarely	Meryl is on a diet. She *rarely* eats dessert.
seldom	Jeff *seldom* goes to bed before midnight. He is *seldom* tired before midnight.
never (0% of the time)	Suzanne is a vegetarian. She *never* eats meat.

A Add a frequency adverb that makes each sentence true for you.

1. I _____ get up early.

2. I _____ eat breakfast with my parents.

3. I _____ take the bus to school.

4. I _____ take a nap in the afternoon.

5. I _____ make my own meals.

6. I am _____ asleep before midnight.

7. I _____ get enough sleep at night.

8. I _____ watch TV in the evening.

9. I am _____ tired after school.

10. I _____ take a walk after dinner.

B Compare your sentences with a partner's. How many of them are the same?

USING *BEFORE* AND *AFTER*

Before and *after* are prepositions that can be used with nouns; for example, *before school*. You can also combine sentences with *before* and *after* to show time order.

I go to bed. I brush my teeth.   I eat lunch. I take a nap.

Before *I go to bed*, I brush my teeth.   ***After*** *I eat lunch*, I take a nap.

OR   OR

I brush my teeth ***before*** *I go to bed*.   I take a nap ***after*** *I eat lunch*.

Notice that we use a comma in sentences that start with *before* or *after*.

A **Combine the pairs of sentences using *before*. Use a comma.**

1. I eat dinner. I wash my hands.

_____

2. I watch TV. I do my homework.

_____

3. I do my homework. I go to the gym.

_____

4. I read the newspaper. I eat breakfast.

_____

B **Combine the pairs of sentences using *after*. Use a comma.**

1. I get home from school. I take my dog for a walk.

_____

2. I eat dinner. I wash the dishes.

_____

3. I get to school. I put my backpack in my locker.

_____

4. I read my nephew a story. I put him to bed.

_____

C **Complete the sentences.**

1. After I get dressed in the morning, I _____.

2. After I get to school, I _____.

3. Before I do my homework, I _____.

4. Before I make dinner, I _____.

D **Compare your sentences with a partner's.**

USING TIME ORDER

When you write about your day, you should arrange your sentences by time order. You can use signal words to make the order clear to your reader. Here are some time-order signal words:

First of all   Then   After that   Next   Finally

A   **Read each set of sentences. For each set, write *TS* in front of the topic sentence. Then number the supporting sentences so they are in correct time order. Finally, write the sentences in paragraph form.**

1.   _2_   Then he quickly gets dressed and eats breakfast.

     _TS_   Mehmet's mornings are very busy.

     _3_   At 7:45 he is outside waiting for the school bus.

     _1_   His mother wakes him up at 6:30.

_____

_____

_____

_____

2.   ____   She spends every morning exercising at the gym.

     ____   After she leaves the drama school, she goes to work at a store from 5:00 to 9:00 P.M.

     ____   She takes classes at the drama school in the afternoon.

     ____   Maria is very active during the summer.

_____

_____

_____

_____

3. ____ At 6:00 A.M. he goes to the flower market.

____ Mr. Park owns a busy flower shop.

____ After he buys his flowers, he works in his shop from 9:00 to 4:00.

____ When the store closes, Mr. Park delivers flowers.

_____

_____

_____

_____

B Read the paragraph "Relaxing on Sundays" and complete the exercise.

Relaxing on Sundays

I look forward to Sundays, when I have lots of free time. I get up early and make my own breakfast. After breakfast, I usually read the funnies to my little brother. I sometimes call my best friend on the telephone to make plans for the movies we want to see. I practice on my guitar until lunchtime. Then I watch sports on TV or play my new CDs. After dinner, I meet my friend at the movie theater. I try to be in bed before eleven o'clock. I like to relax on Sunday so that I am ready to start my week on Monday.

1. Draw a circle around the topic sentence of the paragraph.

2. Underline the supporting sentences.

3. Draw a circle around the concluding sentence of the paragraph.

C Rewrite the paragraph "Relaxing on Sundays." Change *I* to *Rafael* in the first sentence. Make all necessary changes.

Rafael looks forward to Sundays, when he has lots of free time.

_____

_____

_____

_____

_____

_____

PREWRITING

A Talk to a partner. Ask and answer these questions. Use the words in the Word Bank to help you.

1. Where do you go to school? _____

2. What is your typical school day like? _____

3. How do you get to school? _____

4. What hours do you study? _____

Word Bank

do exercises	get ready for bed	make the bed
do homework	get up	practice an instrument
do the dishes	go to bed	take a shower/bath
do the laundry	go to school	wake up
get dressed/ undressed	make breakfast/lunch/ dinner	

B Draw simple pictures that show what you do on a typical weekday. Write a sentence to go with each picture. The first one has been done for you.

1. *I wake up at 7 A.M. every morning.*
2. _____
3. _____

4. _____
5. _____
6. _____

WRITING

Use your sentences from page 50 to write a paragraph about a typical day in your life. Complete the following sentence and use it as your topic sentence. Use at least three adverbs of frequency in your paragraph. Add a concluding sentence at the end.

During the week, my days are very _____

(busy/boring/interesting)

_____

_____

_____

_____

_____

_____

_____

REVISING

A Exchange paragraphs with a partner. Read your partner's paragraph and check *yes* or *no* for each question on the Paragraph Checklist. Then help your partner improve his/her paragraph.

PARAGRAPH CHECKLIST	YES	NO
1. Is the first word of the paragraph indented?	❏	❏
2. Does each sentence begin with a capital letter and end with a period?	❏	❏
3. Does the paragraph have a topic sentence?	❏	❏
4. Are the sentences in correct time order?	❏	❏
5. Are there at least three adverbs of frequency?	❏	❏

B Use your partner's suggestions to revise your paragraph. Copy it onto a separate piece of paper. Give it the title "A Typical Day in My Life" and put it in your portfolio.

Using Your Imagination

CAN'T YOU DO
ANYTHING RIGHT?

Copyright 2003 by Randy Glasbergen.   www.glasbergen.com

GLASBERGEN

A **Discuss the cartoon with your classmates.**

1. Where does this scene take place?

2. Why do you think the man is frustrated?

3. Do you think the cartoon is funny? Why or why not?

B **Write a paragraph about the typical workday of the man shown in the cartoon.**

You Be the Editor

Read the paragraph "A Busy Doctor." It has five mistakes in prepositions of time. With a partner, find the mistakes and correct them. Cross out the mistakes and write the correct preposition above each one.

A Busy Doctor

Dr. Gary Lesneski is an obstetrician. An obstetrician is a doctor who delivers babies. Dr. Lesneski usually gets up on 6:30 at the morning. He goes to his office at 7:00. His workdays are never typical, but they are always busy. He never knows what time a baby will decide to be born. Sometimes babies are born at the afternoon. Sometimes they are born in night. Often he has to go to the hospital in the middle of the night. He rarely sleeps through an entire night without any interruptions. Dr. Lesneski loves his work, but he looks forward to his vacation on August.

WRITING A MESSAGE ON A CARD

Do you like to send cards to your friends and family?

Look at the front of these cards. Write a two- or three-sentence message on the inside to someone you know.

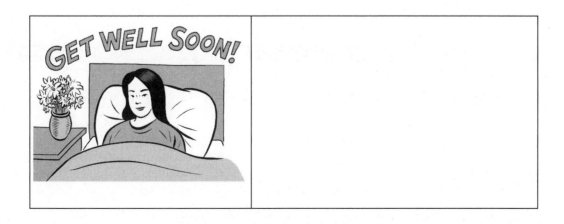

Writing Descriptions

A Look at the people in the pictures. Match the description to the correct picture. Write the correct letter under each picture. Use the words in the Word Banks on the next page to help you.

1. _____ 2. _____ 3. _____ 4. _____ 5. _____

a. Mr. Wilcox is a tall, thin middle-aged man. He is bald but has a black mustache. He wears big glasses. He is wearing a blue jacket and a striped tie. He is carrying a briefcase and an umbrella.

b. Sally is a slender young woman of average height. She has long straight blond hair with bangs that touch the top of her glasses. She is wearing a short wool skirt with a V-neck sweater and leather boots.

c. Dennis is a short young man with a round face and curly red hair. He has big brown eyes, freckles, and a dimple in his chin. He is wearing his favorite T-shirt and shorts. He has a backpack.

d. Tom is a good-looking teenager. He is of average height and weight. He has straight black hair and green eyes. He is wearing a sweatshirt and jeans. He is also wearing a cap and a new pair of white sneakers.

e. Juanita is an attractive young woman. She has long wavy brown hair and big beautiful eyes. Today she's got her hair in a ponytail. She is wearing a striped pantsuit and a black turtleneck. She's got on a silver necklace and long earrings.

Physical Characteristics Word Bank	
Age	middle-aged, old, teenaged, young
Build	average, heavy, medium, slender, small, stocky, strong, thin
Eyes	blue, brown, dark, green, hazel
Face	beard, dimple, freckles, mole, mustache
Hair	bald, black, blond, brown, curly, dark, long, ponytail, red, short, straight, wavy
Height	average, short, tall

Clothing and Personal Items Word Bank	
Accessories	baseball cap, belt, coat, glasses, gloves, hat, purse, scarf, umbrella
Clothing	blazer, blouse, dress, jeans, pants, shirt, shorts, skirt, suit, sweater, sweatpants, sweatshirt, T-shirt, turtleneck, vest
Jewelry	bracelet, earrings, necklace, ring, watch
Shoes	boots, pumps, sandals, sneakers, socks

B Write a short description of these people. Use the words in the Word Banks to help you.

1. _____
   _____
   _____
   _____

2. _____
   _____
   _____
   _____

Developing Your Writing Skills

ADJECTIVES

An adjective is a word that modifies a noun or pronoun. An adjective can describe a noun: a *beautiful* day; a *shrill* voice. An adjective can also make the meaning of a noun or pronoun more definite: *three* books; *that* one. Adjectives answer one of three questions: *What kind? Which one?* or *How many?*

When you write descriptions, you should use adjectives. For example, in the sentence "She has long black hair" the words *long* and *black* are adjectives that describe the noun *hair*. They answer the question, "What kind of hair?"

Here are some rules to remember about using adjectives in English:

Rules	Examples
1. Adjectives have the same form when they describe singular or plural nouns.	She is wearing a **new** jacket. They are wearing **new** jackets.
2. Adjectives usually come before nouns.	He has **brown** eyes. They are wearing **old** sneakers.
3. Adjectives can come after the verb *be* and other linking verbs.	His eyes are **brown**. Their sneakers look **old**.

A Underline the adjectives in the descriptions on page 55. Do not include possessive adjectives.

B Read the student's description of her appearance. Underline the adjectives.

   My name is Jenny Marsh. I am tall and thin. I have long black hair and big brown eyes. I wear glasses. Today I am wearing old blue jeans and a soft yellow sweater. I have on a brown belt and white sneakers.

PREWRITING

Answer these questions about yourself.

What color eyes and hair do you have? Are you tall, short, or average height?

_____

WRITING

A Use the answers to the Prewriting questions on page 57 to write a description of yourself on a separate piece of paper. Do not put your name on the paper. Fold your paper in half and give it to your teacher. Your teacher will give your paper to another student, who will try to guess who wrote the description.

B When your partner returns your description to you, copy it on the lines. Add a topic sentence.

My name is _____ . _____

_____

_____

_____

_____

REVISING

A Exchange paragraphs with a partner. Read your partner's paragraph and check *yes* or *no* for each question on the Paragraph Checklist. Then help your partner improve his/her description.

PARAGRAPH CHECKLIST	YES	NO
1. Is the first word of the paragraph indented?	❏	❏
2. Does each sentence begin with a capital letter and end with a period?	❏	❏
3. Does the paragraph have a topic sentence?	❏	❏
4. Are there at least five adjectives to support the topic?	❏	❏

B Use your partner's suggestions to revise your paragraph. Copy it onto a separate piece of paper. Give it the title "What I Look Like" and put it in your portfolio.

One way to develop a paragraph is to use examples to support your topic sentence. Use "For instance" or "For example" when you give an example.

Complete the sentences with examples.

1. Several of my friends are athletic. *For instance,* _____, _____, and _____ are all good at sports.

2. I love to travel. There are many places I want to visit. *For example,* I would love to see _____, _____, and _____.

3. Many inventions have made our lives easier. *For example,* _____, _____, and _____ have all made our day-to-day activities easier.

DESCRIBING SOMEONE'S CHARACTER

A Read the paragraph and talk about the questions that follow with a partner.

I am a very organized person. For example, I keep my closet very neat. All of my clothes and shoes are arranged by color. I also organize the books in my bookcase by topic. I keep my CDs in alphabetical order so that they are always easy to find. I put all of my important papers in a file in my desk so nothing ever gets lost. My sister makes fun of me and says that I am too organized. However, I never lose anything, and my sister is always looking for something.

1. What is the topic sentence?

2. What examples does the author give to support the idea that he/she is an organized person?

B Rewrite the paragraph. Change *I* to *Yoko* in the first sentence. Make all the necessary changes.

Yoko is a very organized person. For example, she _____

_____

_____

_____

_____

PREWRITING

A Think of a person you know well, such as a friend or relative. Circle one adjective from the Word Bank that describes the person.

Word Bank				
ambitious	energetic	honest	organized	serious
artistic	enthusiastic	jealous	patient	shy
boring	friendly	kind	quiet	social
brave	funny	lazy	responsible	studious
competitive	generous	messy	selfish	talkative
creative	hardworking	neat	sensitive	thrifty
dependable	helpful	optimistic		

B Write the topic sentence for a paragraph about the person. Include both the name of the person and the adjective you chose.

EXAMPLE

My brother is a very curious person.

C Make a list of at least three examples that support your topic sentence.

EXAMPLE

He is always asking questions.

1. _____

2. _____

3. _____

WRITING

Use your list as a guide to write a paragraph. Remember to start with your topic sentence. Try to include at least three examples.

_____

_____

_____

_____

_____

REVISING

A Exchange paragraphs with a partner. Read your partner's paragraph and check *yes* or *no* for each question on the Paragraph Checklist. Then help your partner improve his/her description.

PARAGRAPH CHECKLIST	YES	NO
1. Does the paragraph have a topic sentence?	❑	❑
2. Does the topic sentence give the name of the person and an adjective that describes him/her?	❑	❑
3. Are there at least three examples to support the topic?	❑	❑

B Use your partner's suggestions to revise your paragraph. Copy it onto a separate piece of paper. Give it the title "A _____ Person" and put it in your portfolio.

On Your Own

On a separate piece of paper, write a paragraph about your own character, using the Word Bank on page 60. Give at least three examples to support your topic sentence. After your teacher has read your paragraph, copy it over, give it the title "More about Me," and put it in your portfolio.

DESCRIBING THINGS

A Work with a partner. Match the pictures on the next page from the International Gift Shop catalog with the name of the item. Use words from the Word Bank below the pictures. Write the name of the item on the line.

International Gift Shop

1. _____

2. _____

3. _____

4. _____

5. _____

Chinese rug   flowered plate   leather gloves   necklace   Turkish towel

B **Read the description of each item. Circle the adjectives in each description.**

1. This beautiful necklace was made in Korea. It will make a nice gift for a special person. You can order this pretty necklace for $90.

2. These brown leather gloves are made in Brazil and will keep your hands warm in the winter. The gloves are soft and smooth. You can order a pair of these attractive gloves in size small, medium, or large. Buy them for yourself, or give them as a gift for $25.

3. This rectangular silk and wool rug was made by hand in China. It is 3 feet wide and 6 feet long and has a bright geometric pattern. You can own this beautiful rug for a special price of $530.

4. This cotton Turkish towel has an interesting pattern and is very large and soft. It is so thick you will want to use it at home and at the beach. You can order two for only $45.

5. This round plate was hand-painted in Mexico. The beautiful design has flowers and leaves. The bright colors look nice in any room. We are offering it to you for only $20, so order it right away.

The key to writing a good description is using specific details. When you describe what someone or something looks like, use lots of details in the supporting sentences so your readers can form a picture in their minds.

PREWRITING

Find a picture in a magazine or draw a picture of a product from your country. Make a list of words and phrases that describe the product. Use words from the Word Bank to help you with vocabulary.

Description Word Bank	
Opinion	attractive, beautiful, bright, interesting, pretty, soft
Shape	oval, rectangular, square
Design	flowered, geometric, plain, striped
Material	cotton, gold, leather, plastic, silk, silver, wood, wool

Picture of a Product from My Country

_____   _____

_____   _____

_____   _____

_____   _____

_____   _____

Use the list you wrote as a guide to describe your product for the International Gift Shop catalog. Begin with a sentence that gives the name of the product and the country it is from. Use at least five adjectives. Don't forget to include the price of your product.

_____

_____

_____

REVISING

A Exchange your description with a partner. Read your partner's description and check *yes* or *no* for each question on the Paragraph Checklist. Then help your partner improve his/her description.

PARAGRAPH CHECKLIST	YES	NO
1. Is the name of the product and the country it is from stated in the first sentence?	❏	❏
2. Does the description look like the picture of the product?	❏	❏
3. Are there enough adjectives to describe nouns?	❏	❏
4. Are the adjectives in the correct order?	❏	❏
5. Does the paragraph have a topic sentence?	❏	❏
6. Is the price given?	❏	❏

B Use your partner's suggestions to revise your description. Copy it onto a separate piece of paper. Give it the title "A Product from _____" and put it in your portfolio.

On Your Own

Choose a flag that represents a country, a state, or a special organization. Draw a picture of the flag. Write a paragraph that describes what the flag looks like. Include the colors, shapes, design, etc. If any of these things has a special meaning, you can write about that, too. Share your description with your classmates. Give your description a title and put it in your portfolio.

Using Your Imagination

WRITING ABOUT CARS

Study the words in the Word Bank.

Car Parts Word Bank			
Interior			
accelerator	CD player/radio	emergency brake	ignition
airbag	clutch	gearshift	rearview mirror
brake	cruise control	Global Positioning	seatbelt
bucket seat	dashboard	System	steering wheel
Exterior			
bumper	license plate	tire	windshield
gas tank	roof	trunk	windshield
headlight	side mirror	turn signal	wiper
hood	taillight	wheel cover (hubcap)	

A Think about what cars will be like in the future. Use your imagination to write a paragraph about cars of the future. For example, do you think that they will be bigger or smaller? Will they still run on gasoline? What will dashboards look like? Will cars need bumpers? Where will the trunk be? How many tires will cars have? Will humans have to drive them?

B Exchange paragraphs with a partner. Suggest changes that you think will make the paragraph better.

C Rewrite your paragraph on a separate piece of paper. Give it the title "Cars of the Future" and put it in your portfolio.

You Be the Editor

Read the paragraph "A Birthday Gift" on page 66. It has five mistakes in the use of adjectives. With a partner, find the five mistakes and correct them.

My brother's birthday is next week, and I want to buy him a news sweater. In a catalog, I saw one that is made in Canada. I think he will like it. It's a striped sweater blue. My brother has eyes blue, so it will look nice on him. The sweater is made of soft wool, so it is warms. It is a sweater that fits loosely, so it comfortable is to wear. He can wear it to work or on the weekends. I'm so happy I had this idea, and I think my brother will be happy, too!

Real-Life Writing

FILLING OUT AN ORDER FORM

You want to order something from the International Gift Shop catalog on page 62. Complete the order form below.

INTERNATIONAL GIFT SHOP

ORDER TOLL FREE
1–800–371–2311

Send To:
Name _____
Address _____
City _____
State _____ ZIP _____
Country _____

Item Number	Quantity	Item Description	Color	Gift Wrap	Price	Total Price
				Yes/No		

Payment Method	Merchandise Total	
☐ Check ☐ Credit Card	$6.50 Shipping Charge	

Card Account Number | Month Year | TOTAL |

| | | | | | | | | | | | | | | | | | |

Signature _____

Writing about Places

A Look at the picture of a student's bedroom and underline the adjectives in the paragraph "A Cozy Bedroom." Do not underline possessive adjectives.

A Cozy Bedroom

My bedroom is small but cozy. There are two windows, so my room is usually bright and sunny. I have a desk for my computer. All the books I need to use while I am studying are in the bookcase. My bed is across from the desk. It is not big, but it is comfortable. Above the bed, there is a painting of a bowl of fruit that I bought. It's not very good, but I love the bright colors. I also have an old dresser that belonged to my grandmother. There are a couple of photographs of my family on top of it. I enjoy spending time in my bedroom.

B Look at the pictures of the three bedrooms on the next page. In small groups, discuss each picture and make a list of the things in each room. Use the Word Bank to help you.

Word Bank

bed	closet	hockey stick	phone	tennis racket
bedspread	computer	ice skates	poster	TV
bookcase	curtains	lamp	rug	vase
books	desk	nightstand	skis	VCR
chair	dresser	paintbrushes	slippers	wastebasket
clock	easel	painting	stereo	window

Room 1

_____

_____

_____

_____

_____

Room 2

_____

_____

_____

_____

_____

Room 3

_____

_____

_____

_____

_____

C What adjectives would you use to describe each room? Use the Word Bank to help you. Try to add some other words.

Word Bank		
clean	messy	organized
cluttered	neat	small
cozy	orderly	sunny
large		

Room 1   **Room 2**   **Room 3**

messy
_____   _____   _____

_____   _____   _____

_____   _____   _____

Developing Your Writing Skills

THERE IS AND THERE ARE

When you describe a place, you can use *there is* and *there are*. Look at these rules and examples:

Rules	Examples
1. Use ***there is*** with singular nouns.	***There is*** a big window in the classroom. ***There is*** one computer in the principal's office.
2. Use ***there are*** with plural nouns.	***There are*** lots of windows in the classroom. ***There are*** many computers in the library.
3. The <u>subject</u> comes after the verb.	***There is*** a <u>dictionary</u> on the table. ***There are*** <u>some books</u> on the table.

A Underline the sentences with *there is* and *there are* in the paragraph "A Cozy Bedroom" on page 68.

B Work with a partner. Write two sentences about each of the rooms on page 69 using *there is* or *there are*.

Room 1

1. _____

2. _____

Room 2

1. _____

2. _____

Room 3

1. _____

2. _____

PARAGARAPH POINTER	Prepositions of Place

When you want to explain where something is located, you need to use the correct preposition. The prepositions below will help you describe where items are located in relation to other items.

above	beside	in	in front of	on
behind	between	in back of	next to	under

A Look at the pictures. Then complete the sentences with the correct prepositions from the list above.

1. There are three pictures _____ the couch. The coffee table is _____ the couch. There are some flowers _____ the vase _____ the coffee table.

2. There are lots of books _____ the bookcase. The fax machine
is _____ a table _____ the bookcase and desk.
There is a computer _____ the desk. The wastebasket is
_____ the desk.

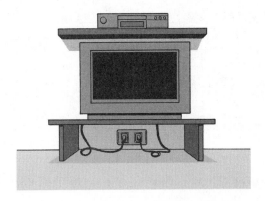

3. The DVD player is _____ the shelf _____ the TV.
There is an electrical outlet _____ the TV.

B **Look at the picture on page 73. Practice using prepositions of place by
adding each new item to the picture. Then compare your picture with one
of your classmates' pictures.**

1. Draw a bowl of fruit in front of the grandmother.

2. Draw a rug under the table.

3. Draw a toy next to the father's chair.

4. Draw a clock on the wall behind the grandfather.

5. Draw a vase between the candles on the table.

6. Draw a flower in the vase.

7. Draw a cake on the long table behind the daughter.

8. Draw a painting on the wall above the long table.

When you write a paragraph, all of the sentences must support the main idea stated in the topic sentence. This is called paragraph unity. Do not include sentences that do not relate to the topic sentence.

A   **Read the paragraph.**

Our garage has become the family's storage center. In one corner we keep boxes of old books and magazines that we plan to give to the library. Under a table that holds my father's toolbox, we have an old computer, a vacuum cleaner that needs to be repaired, some lamps that have to be rewired, and a tricycle missing its third wheel. Next to that table, my mother stores our barbecue grill and a spare set of dishes. We often have to park our car in the driveway. Against the back wall my sister has stacked large oil paintings that need to be framed before she can sell them. There's hardly any room for my bicycle or my brother's moped.

All of the sentences except one support the main idea stated in the topic sentence. The fact that the car needs to be parked in the driveway does not relate to the idea that the garage has become a storage center. It should not be included in the paragraph.

B Now, read the paragraph "A Messy Bedroom" and underline the topic
sentence. Then find the two sentences that do not support the main idea
and cross them out.

A Messy Bedroom

My brother's bedroom is always messy. For example, he rarely makes
his bed or hangs up his clothes. There are usually piles of clothes on
the floor and chair. His schoolbooks and papers are all over his desk.
His favorite book is *One Hundred Years of Solitude*. The top of his
dresser is covered with CDs, soda cans, and magazines. I bought the
dresser for him at a used-furniture store. I wish he would clean up his
room!

PREWRITING

A Think about your bedroom. Describe it to a partner. Discuss the things you
like and don't like about your room. Ask and answer the questions.

1. What size is your room?

2. What adjectives would you use to describe it?

3. What pieces of furniture do you have in your room?

4. Are there any windows? Is it sunny or dark?

5. Do you like your room? Why or why not?

B Draw a simple picture of your room.

WRITING

Write a paragraph that describes your room. Use at least three prepositions of place. Also write at least one sentence with *there is* and one sentence with *there are*. Remember to begin with a topic sentence.

_____

_____

_____

_____

_____

_____

_____

_____

_____

_____

REVISING

A Exchange paragraphs with a partner. Read your partner's paragraph and check *yes* or *no* for each question on the Paragraph Checklist. Then help your partner improve his/her paragraph.

PARAGRAPH CHECKLIST	YES	NO
1. Does the paragraph begin with a topic sentence?	❏	❏
2. Does the paragraph have enough details?	❏	❏
3. Does the paragraph include sentences with *there is* and *there are*?	❏	❏
4. Are there at least three prepositions of place?	❏	❏
5. Are there any sentences that do not belong?	❏	❏

B Use your partner's suggestions to revise your paragraph. Copy it onto a separate piece of paper. Give it the title "My Room" and put it in your portfolio.

Read the letter.

January 2

Dear Carmen,

We just moved into our new apartment. It's on the second floor of a building near a park. The thing I like most about the apartment is that it's very sunny. There are big windows in every room. It has a large living room with a fireplace. There are bookcases on two walls. The kitchen is small, but the appliances are new. There is a long hall next to the kitchen that leads to the bedrooms and bathroom. There is new carpeting in the bedrooms. The only problem is that the closet in my bedroom is very small. I can't wait for you to visit me.

Love,
Sema

PREWRITING

Think about the place where you live. Describe your house, apartment, or room to a partner. Discuss the things you like and don't like about the place. Ask and answer these questions:

1. Where do you live?

2. How many rooms do you have? What size are the rooms?

3. Is your home old or new?

4. Is it sunny or dark? Are there lots of windows?

5. Do you like your home? Why or why not?

WRITING

Write about your home in a letter to a friend or relative in the space below. Use the letter on page 76 as a guide.

_____ (date)

Dear_____,

Love,

_____

REVISING

After your teacher has read your letter, use any suggestions to revise it. Copy it onto a separate piece of paper. Give it the title "My Home" and put it in your portfolio.

WRITING ABOUT YOUR HOMETOWN

Read the paragraph "My Hometown" on page 78 and cross out the sentence that doesn't belong.

My Hometown

I am from Vancouver, a large city in the southwest corner of Canada near the Pacific Ocean. Vancouver is a beautiful city that is surrounded by water and mountains. Vancouver has a mild climate, even in winter. Now I live in Florida, and it is often very hot and humid. Vancouver is an important center for business. It is the busiest port city in Canada, and it is a center of mining, software, and biotechnology. We also have a huge tourist industry. Vancouver is safe and clean, and it has natural beauty as well as many historic, cultural, and recreational opportunities. I love my city and I think you will, too. Please come visit Vancouver!

PREWRITING

A Describe your hometown to a partner. Use the words in the Word Bank to help you.

Word Bank		
architecture	crime	polluted
bridges	cultural attractions	population
capitol	industry	port
city	modern	safe
clean	night life	sports
climate	parks	town

B Make a list of the information about your hometown that you want to include in your paragraph.

_____

_____

_____

_____

_____

_____

_____

WRITING

Complete the topic sentence. Then use the information on your list to write a paragraph. Try to include at least three adjectives in your paragraph.

My hometown, _____ , is a _____ place.

_____

_____

_____

_____

_____

_____

REVISING

A Exchange paragraphs with a partner. Read your partner's paragraph and check *yes* or *no* for each question on the Paragraph Checklist. Then help your partner improve his/her paragraph.

PARAGRAPH CHECKLIST	YES	NO
1. Does the paragraph begin with a topic sentence?	❏	❏
2. Does the paragraph have enough details?	❏	❏
3. Are there at least three adjectives?	❏	❏
4. Are there any sentences that do not belong?	❏	❏

B Use your partner's suggestions to revise your paragraph. After your teacher has read your paragraph, copy it onto a separate piece of paper. Give it the title "My Hometown" and put it in your portfolio.

WRITING A LETTER

A Write a letter to a friend who is coming to visit you. Make a list of the places to go and things to do.

Places to Go	Things to Do
_____	_____
_____	_____
_____	_____
_____	_____

B The letter has been started for you. Complete the beginning of the letter and then finish it.

_____ (date)

Dear _____,

    I was so happy when you called to tell me you were planning to come to _____ to visit me. There are lots of places to go and things to see and do here. We can _____ _____. _____

_____

_____

_____

_____

_____

                            Love,

                            _____

DESCRIBING A PICTURE

A Write three sentences that describe the photograph. Use a preposition in each sentence.

1. _____

2. _____

3. _____

B Use the sentences you wrote to write a description of the picture.

_____

_____

_____

_____

_____

_____

Using Your Imagination

WRITING A HAIKU

Haiku is a very old form of poetry from Japan. Haiku poems are usually about nature. The form of a haiku is always the same. It contains three lines:

The first line has five syllables.

The second line has seven syllables.

The third line has five syllables.

Here are some examples that students have written.

Look up in the sky
See the blue birds flying high
Over the ocean

        —Vasakorn Bhadranavik

Noisy rain has stopped
White snow covers everything
Silent night has come

        —Kazu Karasawa

The birds of passage
Are taking a winter's rest
Ready to go south

    —Fumihiko Suita

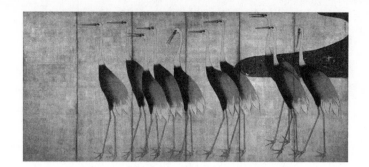

A Choose a season and a scene from nature that you would like to write about. Think about the picture that you want to create in your readers' minds. Then follow the steps in Exercise B to write your own haiku.

Season: _____

Scene from nature: _____

_____

B 1. Decide what your first line will be. Work on the words until you have exactly five syllables. Write it on the first line in the box.

2. Write your second line. Remember that it must contain seven syllables.

3. Write your third line. Make sure it contains five syllables.

My Haiku

C Exchange your haiku with a partner. Make sure you understand your partner's haiku. Make sure the syllable count is correct for each line.

D Rewrite your haiku on a separate sheet of paper. Illustrate your haiku with photographs or drawings and display it in your classroom. When your haiku is returned to you, give it the title "My Haiku" and put it in your portfolio.

Read the paragraph "A Popular Place to Vacation." It has five mistakes in the use of *there is* and *there are*. With a partner, find the mistakes and correct them. There is also one sentence that does not belong. Find the sentence and cross it out.

A Popular Place to Vacation

Honolulu is a great place to go for a family vacation because there is many things to do and see. First of all, there is beautiful beaches that are perfect for people who like water sports. For example, Waikiki Beach is one of the most famous surfing areas in the world. Surfing can be dangerous. The hikers in your family will find lots of challenges. For instance, there are a big volcano called Diamond Head that is right in Honolulu. The view from the top of Diamond Head is spectacular. The shopping is also fabulous. Many stores there are to choose from. Some members of your family might enjoy going to a hula show or a luau dinner in the evening. It is also an aquarium you can visit. It's no wonder that Hawaii is one of the most popular vacation destinations in the world.

Real-Life Writing

ADDRESSING AN ENVELOPE

A Look at the sample envelope.

Toby Boxer
52 Walden Street
Ames, IA 50010

Ms. Charlotte Brown
234 Benefit Street
Providence, RI 02912

B Address the envelope for your letter to your friend on page 80. Put your name and address in the upper left corner. Then put the person's name and address in the middle.

WRITING A POSTCARD

A Read the postcard that was sent from Rio de Janeiro, Brazil. It shows the correct form for writing and addressing a postcard.

Dear Aya,

Rio de Janeiro is awesome! We spent yesterday on Ipanema Beach. Rio is the city that never sleeps, especially during Carnaval! You must see this place before you go back home to Japan.

See you soon.

Love,
Muriel

Ms. Aya Ochiai
551 West Cedar Street
Ann Arbor, MI 48105

B Use the space below to draw a simple picture that shows a place you have visited. Then write a message to a friend or relative. Address the postcard correctly.

CHAPTER
7

Writing Instructions

Getting Ready to Write Steps in a Process

A Look at the six pictures. They show the steps involved in making a yogurt milkshake. Find the sentence from the list below that goes with each picture. Match the sentence to the correct picture.

1. _____

2. _____

3. _____

4. _____

5. _____

6. _____

a. Then cut up some fresh fruit such as bananas, peaches, mangoes, or strawberries.

b. First, get out one cup of yogurt, two cups of milk, and two tablespoons of honey.

c. Add the fruit to the yogurt, milk, and honey in the blender.

d. Pour the yogurt, milk, and honey into a blender.

e. Finally, pour the milkshake into glasses and enjoy your nutritious snack.

f. Put the top on the blender, set on medium, and blend for two minutes.

B Use the sentences to complete a paragraph about how to make a yogurt milkshake.

How to Make a Yogurt Milkshake

When you want a delicious and healthy snack, try this yogurt milkshake.

_____

_____

_____

_____

_____

_____

_____

Developing Your Writing Skills

PLURAL NOUNS

Most English nouns have a singular and plural form. Study the charts to see how to form plural nouns.

FORMING THE PLURAL OF NOUNS

Type of Noun	Forming Plural	Examples
Most nouns	Add an *s*	banana/bananas cup/cups snack/snacks
Nouns that end in *s, ss, x, sh,* and *ch*	Add *es*	campus/campuses class/classes tax/taxes wish/wishes lunch/lunches
Nouns that end in a consonant + *y*	Change the *y* to *i* and add *es*	berry/berries city/cities family/families

There are other rules for the plural forms, but these are the most common:

Type of Noun	Forming Plural	Examples
Nouns that end in *o*	Add *es*	mango/mangoes potato/potatoes tomato/tomatoes volcano/volcanoes
Nouns that end in *f*	Change *f* to *v* and add *es*	half/halves wolf/wolves loaf/loaves Exception: roof/roofs
Nouns that end in *fe*	Change *f* to *v* and add *s*	knife/knives life/lives wife/wives

In addition, there are plural forms that do not follow rules. They are irregular plural nouns:

man/men   woman/women   child/children   person/people

foot/feet   tooth/teeth   mouse/mice   radio/radios

Some words do not change their form. They are spelled the same way in their singular and plural forms:

deer   species

Look at your paragraph "How to Make a Yogurt Milkshake" and underline the plural nouns.

PARAGARAPH POINTER   **Organizing Steps in a Process**

When you want to tell someone how to do something, the first thing you need to do is make a list of the steps in the process. Then you should arrange the steps according to time order. When you write your paragraph, use signal words to make the order of the steps clear to the reader. Here are some examples of time-order signal words:

first, second, third   then   next
first of all   after that   finally

Complete the paragraphs using time-order signal words.

1. It is easy to get a good picture of your cat if you follow these steps.
    _____, give your cat something to eat. When she is full, move
    your cat to a sunny window. _____, rub your cat's back for a
    few minutes until she falls asleep. Do not make any loud noises. As soon as
    she wakes up, get in position and have your camera ready.
    _____, take the picture as she yawns and stretches.

2. In order to get a driver's license in the United States, you need to follow
    these steps. _____, go to the Department of Motor Vehicles in
    the state where you live and fill out an application. _____,
    study for and take a written test on the traffic signs and driving laws. You
    also have to take and pass a vision test. _____, take a road
    test with an examiner who will make sure that you can drive safely. Once you
    pass the road test, you will get your driver's license.

IMPERATIVE SENTENCES

When you tell someone how to do something, you can use imperative sentences.
Imperative sentences begin with the base form of a verb and end with a period.
Imperative sentences are different from regular sentences because they do not
have a subject. Look at the examples. Notice that each one begins with a verb.

> EXAMPLES
>
> **Give** your cat something to eat.
> **Go** to the Department of Motor Vehicles in the state where you live and fill
> out an application.

For negative imperative forms use: *Do + not* (OR *Don't*) + base form of the verb.

> EXAMPLE
>
> **Do not make** any loud noises.

**Look back at your paragraph "How to Make a Yogurt Milkshake" on page 89.
Underline the imperative sentences you used.**

HOW TO FLY A KITE

A With a partner, discuss the pictures. They show how to fly a kite. Read the list of steps that follows and number the steps so they are in the correct order.

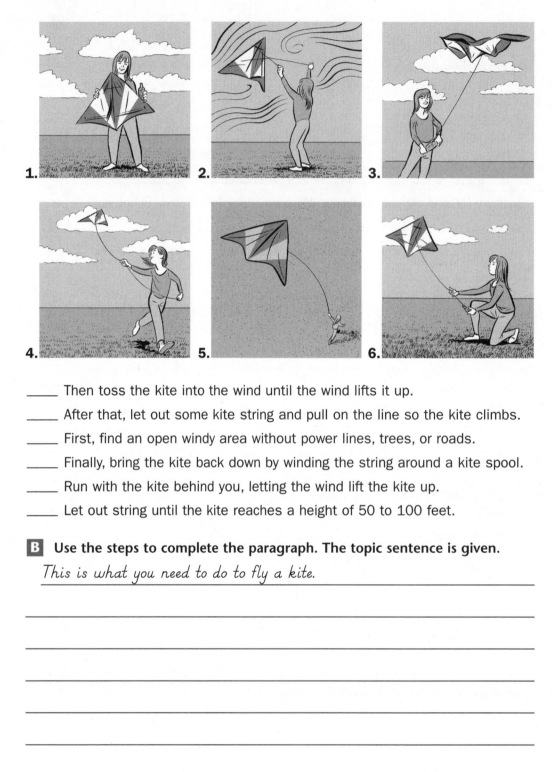

_____ Then toss the kite into the wind until the wind lifts it up.

_____ After that, let out some kite string and pull on the line so the kite climbs.

_____ First, find an open windy area without power lines, trees, or roads.

_____ Finally, bring the kite back down by winding the string around a kite spool.

_____ Run with the kite behind you, letting the wind lift the kite up.

_____ Let out string until the kite reaches a height of 50 to 100 feet.

B Use the steps to complete the paragraph. The topic sentence is given.

This is what you need to do to fly a kite. _____

_____

_____

_____

_____

_____

_____

HOW TO CLEAN SILVER JEWELRY

A Look at the six pictures. They show how to clean silver jewelry. Write a sentence for each picture.

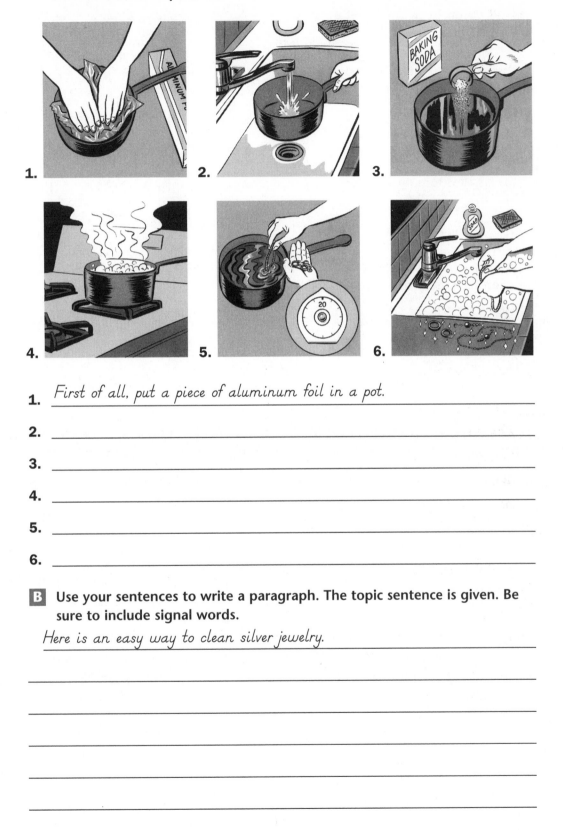

1. *First of all, put a piece of aluminum foil in a pot.*

2. _____

3. _____

4. _____

5. _____

6. _____

B Use your sentences to write a paragraph. The topic sentence is given. Be sure to include signal words.

Here is an easy way to clean silver jewelry.

_____

_____

_____

_____

_____

A Choose one of the topics to write about.

- How to give your pet a bath

- How to pack for a weekend trip

- How to make a good salad

- How to wrap a gift

- How to install software on a computer

- How to cure the hiccups

- How to treat a cold

- How to convert from Celsius to Fahrenheit or metric to American measurements

B Make a list of all the steps in the process. Be sure to put the steps in the correct time order.

_____

_____

_____

_____

_____

_____

_____

_____

WRITING

On the next page, write a paragraph giving instructions. Use the list of steps as a guide. Remember to begin with a topic sentence that states the process you are describing. Also be sure to include some signal words to help guide your reader.

_____

_____

_____

_____

_____

_____

REVISING

A Exchange paragraphs with a partner. Read your partner's paragraph and check *yes* or *no* for each question on the Paragraph Checklist. Then help your partner improve his/her instructions.

PARAGRAPH CHECKLIST	YES	NO
1. Is there a topic sentence?	❏	❏
2. Are the sentences in the correct time order?	❏	❏
3. Are there signal words to help guide the reader?	❏	❏

B Write a title for your paragraph. Share your paragraph with your classmates. Put your instruction paragraph in your portfolio.

On Your Own

Choose one of the topics and write a process paragraph on a separate piece of paper. Give your paragraph a title and put it in your portfolio.

- How to clean something (for example, your room, the garage)

- How to fix something (for example, a flat tire, a broken vase)

- How to cook or bake something

- How to play something (for example, checkers, soccer)

- One of the other paragraph topics from the list on page 94

You Be the Editor

Read the paragraph "Making a Snowplow Turn on Skis." It has six mistakes in singular and plural nouns. With a partner, find the mistakes and correct them.

Making a Snowplow Turn on Skis

The first steps in controlling your speed and direction in skiing is making a snowplow, or wedge, turns. Begin by spreading your foot apart about shoulder width, keeping your knees and ankle slightly bent. Point your toes in so that the tip of your skis point toward each other. Use your legs, hips, and feet, not your shoulders and upper body. To turn left, put pressure on the inside edge of the right skis. To turn right, push down on the inside of the left ski. As you finish the turn, release pressure on the edge of the ski. Then get ready for the next turn.

Real-Life Writing

WRITING A RECIPE CARD

A Write a recipe card for one of your favorite dishes. Fill out the recipe card. First, make a list of the ingredients. Then write the instructions for how to prepare the dish. Use the words in the Word Bank to help you.

			Word Bank		
bake	chop	cut	grill	mix	sauté
boil	combine	fry	heat	peel	simmer
broil	cook	garnish	melt	pour	stir

_____
(name of dish)

Ingredients: _____

_____

_____

_____

_____

Instructions: _____

_____

_____

B Prepare the dish and bring it to class to share with your classmates. Put your recipe card in your portfolio.

CHAPTER 8

Writing a Narrative

Getting Ready to Write a Story

Read the story "My Vacation in a National Park" and number the pictures so they tell the story in the correct time order.

My Vacation in a National Park

My brother and I had an exciting vacation in Yosemite National Park last winter. When we arrived, we unpacked in a comfortable room in a lodge near Yosemite Falls. Then we changed our clothes and went to the Badger Pass ski area. That evening after dinner we relaxed in front of a cozy fire. The next day a National Park Ranger led us on a tour of the Valley Floor and told us about the rock formations, the plants, and the animals in the park. Yosemite Park is truly a winter wonderland. The mountaintops and trees looked very beautiful. Later that night we skated at an outdoor rink under a full moon. On our last day we learned how to snowboard. It was so much fun that I decided to visit Yellowstone National Park next winter.

_____

_____

_____

_____

_____

_____

PAST TENSE VERBS

To form the past tense of regular verbs, add *ed* to the base form. For example: pack—pack**ed**

Study the spelling rules below for forming the past tense of regular verbs.

Rules	Examples

1. For verbs ending in:
 	
    one vowel + *y,*
    two consonants   } add *ed*
    two vowels + one consonant
	enjoy—enjoyed
	walk—walked
	need—needed

2. For verbs ending in a consonant + *e*, add *d*	arrive—arrived
3. For verbs ending in a consonant + *y*, change the *y* to *i* and add *ed*	study—studied
4. For verbs ending in one vowel + one consonant, double the final consonant and add *ed*	plan—planned

Many common verbs in English are irregular. Study these past tense forms of irregular verbs.

Verb	Past Tense Form	Verb	Past Tense Form
become	became	lead	led
begin	began	leave	left
bring	brought	make	made
build	built	say	said
come	came	see	saw
drive	drove	sell	sold
fall	fell	speak	spoke
find	found	spend	spent
fly	flew	take	took
get	got	teach	taught
give	gave	tell	told
go	went	think	thought
have	had	wake	woke

Note: Refer to Appendix 2 on page 135 for an additional list of irregular verbs and their past tense forms.

A Underline the past tense verbs in "My Vacation in a National Park" on page 99.

B Read the paragraph "A Computer Revolution" and fill in the blanks with the correct past tense of the verb. Compare your answers with a partner's.

A Computer Revolution

Early computers were very different from the computers you use today. They were very big, expensive, and difficult to use. In 1976, everything _____ (change). That year two young friends
1.

named Steve Wozniak and Steve Jobs _____ (invent)
2.

something new and _____ (start) a computer revolution.
3.

They _____ (design) and _____ (build) the
4.   5.

first small, inexpensive personal computer. They _____
6.

(call) it the Apple I. They _____ (sell) 600 Apple I
7.

computers for $666 apiece. The next year, the two Steves

_____ (develop) the Apple II. It was one of the first
8.

personal computers with color graphics and a keyboard. The Apple II

was a huge success. It _____ (make) computer history
9.

because it was the first easy-to-use personal computer. Steve Jobs

_____ (believe) in bringing computer technology to
10.

everyone, and the Apple II soon _____ (begin) turning up
11.

in business offices, schools, and homes everywhere.

PARAGARAPH POINTER **Narrative Paragraphs**

> A narrative paragraph tells a story about something that happened in the past. When you write a narrative paragraph, use time order to organize your sentences.

Read the paragraph "My Trip to Chicago." The story does not make sense because the sentences are not in the right order. Rewrite the story so that the sentences are in the right order.

My Trip to Chicago

My friend called an ambulance, and it took me to the hospital. On the first day I was there, I fell down on an icy sidewalk and broke my ankle. For the rest of my trip I had to use crutches to get around. Last week I went to Chicago to visit a friend. I spent a whole day in Chicago General Hospital.

_____

_____

_____

_____

_____

_____

_____

PREWRITING

A **Complete the sentences.**

1. One of the _____ (happiest, saddest, scariest, most embarrassing) memories I have of my childhood happened when I was _____ years old.

2. A very _____ thing happened to me on my first day of _____.

3. One summer my friends and I had a(n) _____ experience.

4. My trip to _____ was very _____.

5. One of the most enjoyable evenings I have ever spent was the time _____

_____

B **Talk about each situation with a partner. Describe what happened to you in each situation.**

C Choose a situation you would like to write about. Make a list of the events you want to include in your story. Number the events so they are in the correct time order.

_____

_____

_____

_____

_____

_____

_____

WRITING

Write a story based on the situation you chose. Use one of the sentences from Exercise A on page 102 as your topic sentence. Then use your list as a guide to write the supporting sentences. Write your story in the past tense. Make sure that the sentences are in the correct time order. Give your story a title.

_____

_____

_____

_____

_____

_____

_____

_____

REVISING

A Exchange paragraphs with a partner. Read your partner's story and check *yes* or *no* for each question on the Paragraph Checklist. Then help your partner improve his/her paragraph.

PARAGRAPH CHECKLIST

	YES	NO
1. Is there a topic sentence?	❑	❑
2. Are the sentences in the correct time order?	❑	❑
3. Are the past tense verbs in the correct form?	❑	❑

B Use your partner's suggestions to revise your paragraph. Copy your story onto a separate piece of paper. Share it with your classmates and put it in your portfolio.

Using Your Imagination

A Look at the photo of a traffic jam. Talk about the photo with a partner.

B Write a story based on this photo of a traffic jam. Imagine that you are in one of the cars. Tell your reader the time and place of your story in the first sentence. Tell what happened in the next few sentences. Use the past tense.

_____

_____

_____

_____

_____

_____

C Exchange paragraphs with another student. Read your partner's story. If necessary, revise your story. Give it the title "A Traffic Jam" and put it in your portfolio.

Writing a Biography

PREWRITING

A Look at the time line of important events in the life of scientist Marie Curie, the only woman to win two Nobel Prizes.

1867	1891	1895	1903	1906	1911	1914	1934
Was born Maria Sklodowska in Warsaw, Poland	Moved to Paris and began study of mathematics, physics, and chemistry at the Sorbonne	Married scientist Pierre Curie, who worked with her on radioactive materials	Shared the Nobel Prize for Physics for research in radiation phenomena	After husband's death, took his place as Professor of Physics and became first woman to teach at the Sorbonne	Received Nobel Prize for Chemistry for isolating radium	During World War I, created mobile X-ray vans for treatment of wounded soldiers	Died of leukemia, brought on by exposure to radiation in her work

B Write at least one complete sentence for each fact on the time line.

1. _Marie Curie was born Maria Sklodowska in Warsaw, Poland, in 1867._

2. _____

3. _____

4. _____

5. _____

6. _____

7. _____

8. _____

USING TIME EXPRESSIONS

When you write sentences about events on a time line, try to use a variety of time expressions. Look at the examples in the paragraph.

> **In 1903** Marie Curie became the first woman to receive a Nobel Prize. **A few years later,** she became the first woman professor at the Sorbonne in France. **By 1911** she had become the only woman to be honored with two Nobel Prizes.

Look back at the sentences you wrote about Marie Curie. Add expressions of time.

WRITING

Use your sentences to complete the paragraph about Marie Curie. The topic sentence is given.

Marie Curie was a pioneer in the field of radiology.

_____

_____

_____

_____

_____

_____

_____

REVISING

A Exchange paragraphs with a partner. Read your partner's paragraph and check *yes* or *no* for each question on the Paragraph Checklist. Then help your partner improve his/her paragraph.

PARAGRAPH CHECKLIST	YES	NO
1. Is there a topic sentence?	❏	❏
2. Are the sentences in correct time order?	❏	❏
3. Are the past tense verbs in the correct form?	❏	❏
4. Are time expressions used?	❏	❏

B Use your partner's suggestions to revise your paragraph. Copy it onto a separate piece of paper. Give it the title "Marie Curie" and put it in your portfolio.

PREWRITING

A Look at the time line for Seiji Ozawa, a famous Japanese orchestra conductor.

1935	1960	1961–1962	1965–1970	1973–2002	2002
Born in Shenyang, China, to Japanese parents	Won Koussevitsky Prize for outstanding student conductor	Made assistant conductor under Leonard Bernstein of the New York Philharmonic Orchestra	Served as conductor of the Toronto Symphony	Served as director of the Boston Symphony Orchestra, where he stayed until 2002	Appointed music director of the Vienna State Opera

B Write at least one complete sentence for each fact on the time line. Use a variety of time expressions.

1. _____

2. _____

3. _____

4. _____

5. _____

6. _____

C Choose the best topic sentence for a paragraph about Seiji Ozawa. Circle the letter.

a. Seiji Ozawa won a prize for outstanding student conductor in 1960.

b. Seiji Ozawa served as a conductor of the Toronto Symphony.

c. Seiji Ozawa is a famous Japanese orchestra conductor.

WRITING

Write a paragraph about Seiji Ozawa. Begin with the topic sentence you chose.

_____

_____

_____

_____

_____

_____

_____

REVISING

A Exchange paragraphs with a partner. Read your partner's paragraph and check *yes* or *no* for each question on the Paragraph Checklist. Then help your partner improve his/her paragraph.

B Use your partner's suggestions to revise your paragraph. Copy it onto a separate piece of paper. Give it the title "Seiji Ozawa" and put it in your portfolio.

PREWRITING

A Look at the time line for Babe Didrikson Zaharias, who is considered the greatest woman athlete of modern times.

1914	1932	1934	1947	1949	1954
Was born Mildred Didrikson in Port Arthur, Texas	Competed in three events at Olympics, won two gold medals and one silver medal, and broke world record in 80-meter hurdles	A success in every sport, turned to a career in golf	Won seventeen straight amateur victories in golf and decided to turn golf pro	Voted greatest female athlete of the half century by the Associated Press	Made a stunning comeback after undergoing surgery to win U.S. Open by twelve strokes

B Write at least one complete sentence for each fact on the time line.

1. _____

2. _____

(continued)

3. _____

4. _____

5. _____

6. _____

WRITING

Use your sentences to write a paragraph about Babe Didrikson Zaharias. Begin with a topic sentence.

_____

_____

_____

_____

_____

_____

_____

_____

REVISING

A Exchange paragraphs with a partner. Read your partner's paragraph and check *yes* or *no* for each question on the Paragraph Checklist. Then help your partner improve his/her paragraph.

PARAGRAPH CHECKLIST		
	YES	**NO**
1. Is there a topic sentence?	❏	❏
2. Are the sentences in correct time order?	❏	❏
3. Are the past tense verbs in the correct form?	❏	❏
4. Are time expressions used?	❏	❏

B Use your partner's suggestions to revise your paragraph. Copy it onto a separate piece of paper. Give it the title "Babe Didrikson Zaharias" and put it in your portfolio.

Choose one of the famous people to write about. Or choose another person and do some research about him/her. Write a paragraph about the person and share it with your classmates.

Gabriel García Márquez

Name: Gabriel García Márquez

Place of birth: Aracataca, Colombia

Year of birth: 1928

Occupation: Writer

Accomplishments: Published his first book of short stories, *Leaf Storm and Other Stories*, in 1955; wrote the novel *Love in the Time of Cholera* (1985); wrote the non-fiction *News of a Kidnapping* (1996)

Best-known novel: *One Hundred Years of Solitude*, 1967

Prize: Won Nobel Prize for Literature, 1982

Martina Navratilova

Name: Martina Navratilova

Place of birth: Prague, Czechoslovakia

Date of birth: October 18, 1956

Citizenship: Became a U.S. citizen in 1981

Occupation: Professional tennis player

Accomplishments: Was national champion in Czechoslovakia from 1972 to 1975, was top-ranked women's tennis player for many years, won eighteen Grand Slam singles titles and forty Grand Slam doubles titles, won women's singles title at Wimbledon a record nine times, inducted into the Hall of Fame in 2000

Writing Your Autobiography

A Make a time line of the important events in your own life.

(time line)

B Talk about your time line with a partner. Ask and answer questions about each other's time line.

C Write at least one complete sentence for each event on your time line.

1. _____

2. _____

3. _____

4. _____

5. _____

6. _____

WRITING

Use your sentences to write a paragraph about yourself. Tell where and when you were born in the topic sentence. Use the past tense.

_____

_____

_____

REVISING

A Exchange paragraphs with a partner. Read your partner's paragraph and check *yes* or *no* for each question on the Paragraph Checklist. Then help your partner improve his/her paragraph.

PARAGRAPH CHECKLIST

		YES	NO
1.	Is there a topic sentence?	❑	❑
2.	Are the sentences in correct time order?	❑	❑
3.	Are the past tense verbs in the correct form?	❑	❑
4.	Are time expressions used?	❑	❑

B Use your partner's suggestions to revise your paragraph. Copy it onto a separate piece of paper. Give it the title "My Autobiography" and put it in your portfolio.

Using Your Imagination

USING POETRY TO WRITE ABOUT MEMORIES

Sometimes it is fun to write a poem about a special memory. Here are some examples of simple memory poems:

> *Lorentza in Monterrey*
> *Four years old*
> *Sitting in a tree*
> *Waiting for my father to come*
>   *home from work*

> *Koichi in Tokyo*
> *Eleven years old*
> *Playing baseball after school*
> *Eating junk food before dinner*

> *Letizia in Forte dei Marmi*
> *Seventeen years old*
> *Playing the guitar*
> *Singing with my friends*

> *Abdullah in Jeddah*
> *Eight years old*
> *Riding a donkey*
> *Getting water for my family*

A **To write this type of memory poem, think back to a specific time in your childhood. Think about how old you were, where you were, and what you were doing. Use the samples as a guide.**

1. On the first line, write your first name and the name of the place where you were.

   _____

2. On the next line, write your age at that time.

   _____

3. On the third line, write exactly what you were doing (use the *ing* form of the verb).

   _____

4. On the last line, give further information about what was going on (use the *ing* form of the verb).

   _____

5. Make any changes that you want to make in your memory poem. Then copy it below.

   _____

   _____

   _____

   _____

B **Write another memory poem.**

_____

_____

_____

_____

C Choose one of your memory poems and read it to your class.

D Copy your memory poem onto a separate piece of paper. Give it the title "My Memory Poem" and put it in your portfolio.

MEMORY DRAWING

A Think of a special memory from your childhood. Do a very simple drawing of that memory on a separate piece of paper.

B Use the ideas in your drawing to write a paragraph about this memory. Copy your paragraph under your drawing. When you are finished, give it the title "A Memory from My Childhood" and put the drawing and the paragraph in your portfolio.

You Be the Editor

Read the paragraph "An Angry Friend." It has six mistakes in past tense verbs. With a partner, find the mistakes and correct them.

An Angry Friend

I remember the time last year when my best friend, Ellen, gets very mad at me. It was cold that morning, and I borrow a sweater from her. By lunchtime it was warmer, so I taked the sweater off. I forget about the sweater and leaved it in the cafeteria. When I go back to get it, it was gone! My friend was furious with me. The sweater was a gift from her old boyfriend. His mother had knit it for her. Ellen was so angry and upset that she didn't speak to me for a week.

WRITING LOST-AND-FOUND MESSAGES

A Read the Lost-and-Found messages.

> **Lost:** Our brown and white beagle dog—lost near the park. His name is Freckles. The family is heartbroken. If you see him, please call 555-2421.

> **Lost:** Locket lost on Peterson Street. It belonged to my mother, and it is very important to me. If you find it, please call Gabriela at 555-5891.

> **Found:** I found a beautiful, hand-knit, red scarf in the cafeteria. E-mail me at DB@school.org if you think it is yours.

B Write your own Lost or Found message.

WRITING ADVERTISEMENTS

A Read the ads for services.

Do you need an experienced baby-sitter? I LOVE KIDS! References available. Call Samantha at 555-7462.

Word Processing. Excellent typing skills, fast, $5.00 per page. E-mail me at wp@pager.com.

Does your house need painting? I am experienced and neat. Reasonable rates. Call Don at 555-4691.

Housecleaner available. Full-time or part-time, honest, dependable. Call me at 555-3647.

B Write your own service advertisement.

Writing Your Opinion

A Look at the pictures below and on the next page. Match the name of the place or form of transportation to the correct picture. Use the words in the Word Bank. Write the correct word under each picture.

Word Bank

airplane	bus	elevator	museum
automobile	church	library	restaurant
bank	concert hall	movie theater	train

1. _____

2. _____

3. _____

4. _____

5. _____

6. _____

7. _____

8. _____

9. _____

10. _____   11. _____   12. _____

B Talk to a partner about where you think cell phones should be banned.

C Read the paragraphs and answer the questions.

1. I think there should be a ban on using cell phones in most public places, in forms of public transportation, and while driving. First of all, I hate having to listen to other people's conversations. I also hate the sound of cell phones ringing while I'm trying to watch a movie, read a book in the library, or listen to a concert. Moreover, the use of cell phones in places like churches is disrespectful. In addition, drivers who talk on a cell phone when they are driving risk having an accident and hurting themselves, their passengers, and other drivers. I believe that laws need to be passed to limit or ban the use of cell phones except in emergency situations.

    a. What is the author's opinion?

    _____

    b. What four reasons does the author give to support his/her opinion?

    _____

    _____

    _____

    _____

2. In my opinion, it is unfair to ban cell phones in public places and in forms of transportation including automobiles. People have a right to use their cell phones since they are paying for the service. Most people remember to turn off their cell phones during movies and concerts and while they are in museums and libraries. Many businesspeople would be seriously affected by a ban since they spend a lot of time traveling and communicate with their clients on cell phones. They need to work while they are on trains or planes and while they are driving. Finally, a cell phone is essential in emergency situations.

a. What is the author's opinion?

_____

. What four reasons does the author give to support his/her opinion?

_____

_____

_____

_____

Developing Your Writing Skills

USING *SHOULD*

Use *should* or *shouldn't* (*should not*) when you are giving or asking for advice or an opinion. Look at the examples of sentences that use *should* to express an opinion.

EXAMPLES

The county **should** purchase the land to make a park.

You **shouldn't** get mad so easily.

Should I wear my gray dress?

I think you **should** take the chemistry course.

You **should not** skip meals.

He **should** exercise every day.

She **should** take a nap. She looks very tired.

In Statements	In Questions	In Negative Statements
You **should** hang the painting there.	**Should** I hang the painting here?	You **shouldn't** (**should not**) hang the painting there.
Reggie **should** try to find a different job.	**Should** Reggie try to find a different job?	Reggie **shouldn't** (**should not**) try to find a different job.

Study these rules for using *should*:

Rules	Examples
1. *Should* is always followed by the base form of the verb.	Maria ***should*** signed the lease immediately. (Wrong) Maria ***should*** sign the lease immediately. (Right)
2. Do not add *s* to *should* even if you are using the third person singular.	My brother ***shoulds*** work harder. (Wrong) My brother ***should*** work harder. (Right)
3. Do not use an infinitive (*to* + base form) after *should*.	You ***should*** to stop smoking. (Wrong) You ***should*** stop smoking. (Right)

A Write sentences giving advice using *should*.

1. John has a toothache.

He should go to a dentist.

2. Matt is late for work.

_____

3. Frieda has an English test tomorrow.

_____

4. Peter has the hiccups.

_____

5. Jong burned his hand.

_____

6. Lisa has a cold.

_____

B Compare your sentences with a partner's. Did you give the same advice?

USING *BECAUSE*

You can use the word *because* to introduce a reason. *Because* answers the question "Why?"

Why is Frieda studying?

Frieda is studying **because** she has an English test tomorrow.

Why is John going to the dentist?

John is going to the dentist **because** he has a toothache.

Answer the questions using *because*.

1. Why do you think cell phones should be banned in public places?

_____

2. Why are you studying English?

_____

3. Why do you think it is important to exercise?

_____

4. Why do you enjoy seeing new places?

_____

5. Why are computers helpful?

_____

PARAGARAPH POINTER   **Stating Your Opinion in a Topic Sentence**

The following useful phrases are often used to introduce opinions that serve as topic sentences:

I believe (that)   In my opinion,   I think (that)   I feel (that)

Write an opinion topic sentence for the five statements in the previous activity.

In my opinion, cell phones should be banned in public places.
_____

1. _____

2. _____

3. _____

4. _____

5. _____

PREWRITING

A State your opinion by completing the sentences with *should* or *should not*. Then share your opinions with a partner.

1. Cell phones _____ be banned in public places.

2. American students _____ have to learn a second language.

3. People _____ use cell phones while they are driving.

4. Scientists _____ use animals for their research.

5. People _____ have to retire when they are sixty-five years old.

6. Governments _____ make the environment their top priority.

7. Driver's education _____ be taught in public schools.

8. Students _____ have to take physical education courses.

9. The custom of tipping _____ be changed.

10. High school students _____ have to wear uniforms.

PARAGARAPH POINTER **Organizing by Order of Importance**

You need to give reasons, examples, or facts to support your opinion. It is helpful to list your supporting details in the order of importance. The following phrases are often used to introduce facts, reasons, and examples:

First of all,	In addition	Secondly,
For one thing,	Another reason	Thirdly,
One reason that	Moreover,	Finally,
Also,	For example,	

B Choose three of the opinions you wrote in the Prewriting exercise and give two or three reasons, examples, or facts to support each one.

a. Opinion: _____

Reason (Example/Fact) 1: _____

_____

Reason (Example/Fact) 2: _____

_____

Reason (Example/Fact) 3: _____

_____

b. Opinion: _____

Reason (Example/Fact) 1: _____

_____

Reason (Example/Fact) 2: _____

_____

Reason (Example/Fact) 3: _____

_____

c. Opinion: _____

Reason (Example/Fact) 1: _____

_____

Reason (Example/Fact) 2: _____

_____

Reason (Example/Fact) 3: _____

_____

WRITING

Choose one of your opinions as the topic for a paragraph. Use the opinion topic sentence you wrote. Then use your reasons, examples, or facts to write supporting sentences. Remember to use signal words.

_____

_____

_____

_____

_____

_____

_____

_____

REVISING

A   Exchange paragraphs with a partner. Read your partner's paragraph and check *yes* or *no* for each question on the Paragraph Checklist on the next page. Then help your partner improve his/her paragraph.

PARAGRAPH CHECKLIST

		YES	NO
1.	Does the topic sentence state the author's opinion?	❏	❏
2.	Are there at least three sentences to support the opinion?	❏	❏
3.	Are the sentences organized according to order of importance?	❏	❏
4.	Does the paragraph include signal words?	❏	❏

B Use your partner's suggestions to revise your paragraph. Copy it onto a separate piece of paper. Give it the title "My Opinion" and put it in your portfolio.

PREWRITING

A Work with a group of three or four students. Make a list of five things people should do to learn English. Write your ideas in the chart. Write complete sentences using *should*.

Ways to Learn English
1. _____
2. _____
3. _____
4. _____
5. _____

B Compare your chart with another group's. Did you have any of the same ideas? Which ones were the same?

WRITING

Complete the paragraph about the best ways to learn English. The topic sentence is given. Use some of the ideas from your chart for the supporting sentences. End your paragraph with a concluding sentence.

I believe that there are several ways to learn English.

_____

_____

_____

_____

_____

REVISING

A Exchange paragraphs with a partner. Read your partner's paragraph and check *yes* or *no* for each question on the Paragraph Checklist. Then help your partner improve his/her paragraph.

PARAGRAPH CHECKLIST	YES	NO
1. Does the topic sentence state the author's opinion?	❑	❑
2. Are there at least three sentences to support the opinion?	❑	❑
3. Is there a concluding paragraph?	❑	❑
4. Are the sentences organized according to order of importance?	❑	❑
5. Does the paragraph include signal words?	❑	❑

B Use your partner's suggestions to revise your paragraph. Copy it onto a separate piece of paper. Give it the title "Learning English" and put it in your portfolio.

PREWRITING

A Look at the pictures of inventions on pages 128 and 129. Match the name of the invention to the correct picture. Use the words in the Word Bank. Write the correct word under each picture.

Word Bank

airplane	computer	telephone
camera	microwave oven	telescope
car	printing press	TV
cell phone		

1. _____

2. _____

3. _____

4. _____

5. _____

6. _____

7. _____

8. _____

9. _____   10. _____

B Work with a partner. Ask and answer these questions.

1. Which invention do you think had the biggest impact on society? Why? What specific reasons can you think of?

2. Which invention do you think has had the least impact on society? Why? What specific reasons can you think of?

WRITING

Write a paragraph about the invention you think has had the biggest impact on society. Support your opinion with at least three reasons.

_____

_____

_____

_____

_____

REVISING

A Exchange paragraphs with a partner. Read your partner's paragraph and check *yes* or *no* for each question on the Paragraph Checklist. Then help your partner improve his/her paragraph.

PARAGRAPH CHECKLIST	YES	NO
1. Does the topic sentence state the author's opinion?	❏	❏
2. Are there at least three sentences to support the opinion?	❏	❏
3. Are the sentences organized according to order of importance?	❏	❏
4. Does the paragraph include signal words?	❏	❏

B Use your partner's suggestions to revise your paragraph. Copy it onto a separate piece of paper. Give it the title "The Most Important Invention" and put it in your portfolio.

Using Your Imagination

GIVING ADVICE

A Read the letter to the Adviser and the Adviser's response. Discuss the situation and the response with a partner.

Dear Adviser

Dear Adviser:

I have a very close friend named Joel, whom I have known since I came to this country. We have been in many of the same classes, and we often study together. We are invited to the same parties, and we share an interest in jazz and skateboarding, but we have never been on a date. Recently, I met an older student who has asked me to be his prom date. When I told Joel, he became angry at me and now is avoiding me. I don't want to lose Joel's friendship, but I think he's being silly. What do you think I should do?

Thank you,

Puzzled

Dear Puzzled:

Joel probably feels hurt because you have chosen to go out with an older boy. Perhaps he thinks you're losing interest in him. You should ask Joel to meet with you and talk about his feelings. Explain that you value his friendship. A good relationship is based on open communication. Joel may not be willing to throw away a good friendship because of one disappointment. Good luck!

Sincerely,

The Adviser

B Write your own letter to the Adviser.

```
┌─────────────────────────────────────────────────────────┐
│  Dear Adviser:                                            │
│      _____        │
│   _____       │
│   _____       │
│   _____       │
│   _____       │
│   _____       │
│   _____       │
│   _____                            │
└─────────────────────────────────────────────────────────┘
```

C Exchange letters with a partner. Write a response to your partner's letter.

```
┌─────────────────────────────────────────────────────────┐
│  Dear_____ :                                    │
│      _____        │
│   _____       │
│   _____       │
│   _____       │
│   _____       │
│   _____       │
│   _____       │
│                                                           │
│  Sincerely,                                               │
│  The Adviser                                              │
└─────────────────────────────────────────────────────────┘
```

D Read and discuss the responses you and your partner wrote to each other's letters.

On Your Own

Write a paragraph giving your opinion on one of these topics:

1. Hotels should/should not allow pets.

2. People should be able to get a driver's license at age 14/15/16/21.

You Be the Editor

The paragraph has five mistakes in the use of *should*. With a partner, find the five mistakes and correct them.

How to Conserve Water

I think more people should to try to conserve water in their everyday lives. We each use 60 gallons (246 liters) of water every day inside our homes! Conserving water is very important to the future of our planet, and it is also a great way to save money and prevent water pollution. There are several things we should can start now to do every day. One thing is to take shorter showers. A shower shoulds only last about four minutes. Another thing is to turn off the water while we soap our hands, brush our teeth, or shave. In addition, we should used the dishwasher only when it is full. This is true for laundry, too. One of the most important things we should to do is fix leaks immediately. Even a small leak wastes a huge amount of water every hour. These ideas are simple and easy, but they can save a lot of money, and they can help save our planet for our kids and grandkids.

WRITING A LETTER TO THE EDITOR

A Read the editorial in today's newspaper about teaching art to children.

> Last week the Board of Education voted to cut art classes from our schools. The Board obviously doesn't understand the importance of art. The Board is right in saying that math, science, history, etc., are important for kids to learn. They are also right in saying that sports are important for kids' health. The Board is wrong, however, to ignore kids' creative side. People need art. Art helps us express ourselves.
>
> Before the members of the School Board make a decision about the education of children, they should educate themselves about the importance of art in our lives. The purpose of our schools is to educate. Is a child educated if he/she is not taught how to make a picture? The purpose of education is to help children become well-rounded adults. Art is a subject worth studying.

B Write a letter to the editor expressing your opinion about teaching art in school. Do you agree with the editorial?

LETTER TO THE EDITOR

Dear Editor:

_____

_____

_____

_____

_____

_____

_____

Yours truly,

A Reader

APPENDIX 1

ALPHABET AND PENMANSHIP

LOWERCASE AND UPPERCASE PRINTED LETTERS

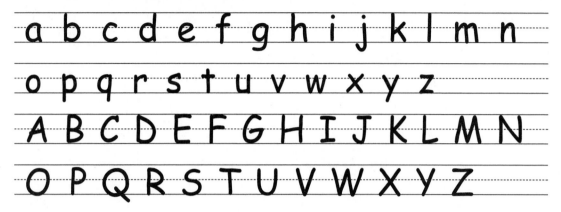

LOWERCASE AND UPPERCASE CURSIVE LETTERS

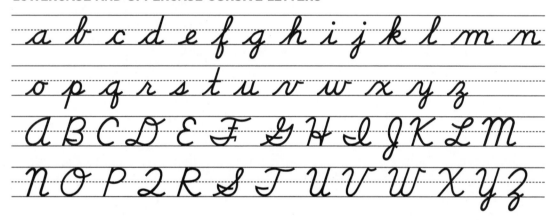

APPENDIX 2

PAST TENSE FORM OF COMMON IRREGULAR VERBS

Most English verbs are regular. Regular verbs add *ed* to form the past tense. English also has many irregular verbs. Following is a list of common irregular verbs.

become/became	find/found	leave/left	speak/spoke
begin/began	fly/flew	make/made	spend/spent
bring/brought	get/got	meet/met	take/took
build/built	give/gave	put/put	teach/taught
buy/bought	go/went	raise/rose	tell/told
come/came	have/had	run/ran	think/thought
do/did	hear/heard	say/said	understand/understood
drive/drove	hit/hit	see/saw	wake/woke
eat/ate	know/knew	sell/sold	win/won
fall/fell	lead/led	sleep/slept	write/wrote
feel/felt			

PUNCTUATION RULES

Punctuation is used to organize written words and guide the reader.

APOSTROPHES

- Use an apostrophe to show possession.

  My car broke down, so I borrowed Jason's.

- Use an apostrophe to write contractions.

  Yuki isn't going to class today.
  Wally can't find his calculator.
  Why weren't you at the game Saturday?

COMMAS

- Use a comma to separate three or more words in a list.

  Maria bought apples, oranges, and blueberries at the store.

- Use a comma to separate the day and year in a date.

  They got married on June 29, 2003.

- Use a comma after the name when you write a letter to a friend.

  Dear Henri,

- Use a comma between the name of a city and a state.

  They live in Austin, Texas.

- Use a comma after the words *yes* and *no* in a sentence.

  Yes, I got your message.

- Use a comma when you use *and*, *but*, or *so* to connect two sentences.

  We will visit my grandmother, and we will also see my aunt.
  Keiko went to the library, but it was closed.
  I lost my book, so I didn't do my homework.

- Use a comma when you **start** a sentence with the words *after, although, because, before, if, since, when,* or *while.*

  Because it was raining, she took an umbrella.
  If he is late again, I will be very angry.
  Since she studies all the time, she is a good student.

- Do **not** use a comma when the words *after, although, because, before, if, since, when,* or *while* are in the **middle** of a sentence.

  She took an umbrella although it wasn't raining.
  We waited outside while he talked to the doctor.
  I had something to eat before I went to the movie.

CHAPTER 1—You Be the Editor (page 10)

A Lucky and Happy Man

My name is Stanley ~~stoico~~ *Stoico*. I am ninety years old. I am from ~~italy~~ *Italy*. I moved to San Diego, ~~california~~ *California*, with my family when I was nine years old. I speak ~~italian~~ *Italian* and ~~English~~ *English*. ~~in~~ *In* my younger years, I had many different jobs. I worked hard and saved my money. In 1955, I started my own business. ~~The~~ *The* business was successful, and ~~i~~ *I* retired in 1983. I like to travel and play golf. I have seen and done a lot in my long life. I am a lucky and happy man.

CHAPTER 2—You Be the Editor (page 24)

My Cousin

My cousin's name is Bettina Lee. She is twenty-seven years old. She was born in Chicago, Illinois, but now ~~her~~ *she* lives in Denver, Colorado. She is married and has two children. Bettina and ~~me~~ *I* enjoy spending time together. ~~Us~~ *We* love to go ice-skating. Bettina is an excellent ice-skater. She skated in ice shows when ~~he~~ *she* was young. Now Bettina teaches ice-skating to young children. She enjoys watching ~~their~~ *them*.

CHAPTER 3—You Be the Editor (page 39)

My Baby Sister

My sister Stephanie is always busy after school. As soon as she ~~get~~ *gets* home, she ~~turnes~~ *turns* on the TV. At the same time, she ~~talk~~ *talks* on the phone to make plans with her best friend. After she ~~watchs~~ *watches* TV and eats a snack, she ~~playies~~ *plays* computer games or IMs her friends for a while. Then she ~~gos~~ *goes* shopping with her friends. No wonder she's too tired to do her homework after dinner.

CHAPTER 4—You Be the Editor (page 52)

A Busy Doctor

Dr. Gary Lesneski is an obstetrician. An obstetrician is a doctor who
delivers babies. Dr. Lesneski usually gets up ~~on~~ *at* 6:30 ~~at~~ *in* the morning. He

goes to his office at 7:00. His workdays are never typical, but they are

always busy. He never knows what time a baby will decide to be born.

Sometimes babies are born ~~at~~ *in* the afternoon. Sometimes they are born
~~in~~ *at* night. Often he has to go to the hospital in the middle of the night. He

rarely sleeps through an entire night without any interruptions. Dr.

Lesneski loves his work, but he looks forward to his vacation ~~on~~ *in* August.

CHAPTER 5—You Be the Editor (page 66)

A Birthday Gift

My brother's birthday is next week, and I want to buy him a ~~news~~ *new*

sweater. In a catalog, I saw one that is made in Canada. I think he will

like it. It's a striped sweater ~~blue~~ *blue*^. My brother has eyes ~~blue~~ *blue*^, so it will

look nice on him. The sweater is made of soft wool, so it is ~~warms~~ *warm*. It

is a sweater that fits loosely, so it *is*^ comfortable ~~is~~ to wear. He can wear

it to work or on the weekends. I'm so happy I had this idea, and I think

my brother will be happy, too!

CHAPTER 6—You Be the Editor (page 84)

A Popular Place to Vacation

Honolulu is a great place to go for a family vacation because there *is* ~~is~~ *are* many things to do and see. First of all, there ~~is~~ *are* beautiful beaches that are perfect for people who like water sports. For example, Waikiki Beach is one of the most famous surfing areas in the world. ~~Surfing can be dangerous.~~ The hikers in your family will find lots of challenges. For instance, there ~~are~~ *is* a big volcano called Diamond Head that is right in Honolulu. The view from the top of Diamond Head is spectacular. The shopping is also fabulous. ~~Many stores there are~~ *There are many stores* to choose from. Some members of your family might enjoy going to a hula show or a luau dinner in the evening. ~~It~~ *There* is also an aquarium you can visit. It's no wonder that Hawaii is one of the most popular vacation destinations in the world.

CHAPTER 7—You Be the Editor (page 96)

Making a Snowplow Turn on Skis

The first ~~steps~~ *step* in controlling your speed and direction in skiing is making a snowplow, or wedge, ~~turns~~ *turn*. Begin by spreading your ~~foot~~ *feet* apart about shoulder width, keeping your knees and ~~ankle~~ *ankles* slightly bent. Point your toes in so that the ~~tip~~ *tips* of your skis point toward each other. Use your legs, hips, and feet, not your shoulders and upper body. To turn left, put pressure on the inside edge of the right ~~skis~~ *ski*. To turn right, push down on the inside of the left ski. As you finish the turn, release pressure on the edge of the ski. Then get ready for the next turn.

CHAPTER 8—You Be the Editor (page 115)

An Angry Friend

I remember the time last year when my best friend, Ellen, ~~gets~~ *got* very

mad at me. It was cold that morning, and I ~~borrow~~ *borrowed* a sweater from her.

By lunchtime it was warmer, so I ~~taked~~ *took* the sweater off. I ~~forget~~ *forgot* about

the sweater and ~~leaved~~ *left* it in the cafeteria. When I ~~go~~ *went* back to get it, it

was gone! My friend was furious with me. The sweater was a gift from

her old boyfriend. His mother had knit it for her. Ellen was so angry and

upset that she didn't speak to me for a week.

CHAPTER 9—You Be the Editor (page 132)

How to Conserve Water

I think more people should ~~to~~ try to conserve water in their everyday

lives. We each use 60 gallons (246 liters) of water every day inside our

homes! Conserving water is very important to the future of our planet,

and it is also a great way to save money and prevent water pollution.

There are several things we should ~~can~~ start now to do every day. One

thing is to take shorter showers. A shower ~~shoulds~~ *should* only last about four

minutes. Another thing is to turn off the water while we soap our

hands, brush our teeth, or shave. In addition, we should ~~used~~ *use* the

dishwasher only when it is full. This is true for laundry, too. One of the

most important things we should ~~to~~ do is fix leaks immediately. Even a

small leak wastes a huge amount of water every hour. These ideas are

simple and easy, but they can save a lot of money, and they can help

save our planet for our kids and grandkids.